THE STAMFORD BRIDGE ENCYCLOPEDIA

Other titles available in the same series

THE STAMFORD BRIDGE ENCYCLOPEDIA

An A-Z of Chelsea FC

Paul Harrison

MAINSTREAM
PUBLISHING

EDINBURGH AND LONDON

First published in Great Britain in 1995 by
MAINSTREAM PUBLISHING COMPANY
(EDINBURGH) LTD
7 Albany Street
Edinburgh EH1 3UG

ISBN 1 85158 749 7

A catalogue record for this book is available from the British
Library

Typeset in Janson by Litho Link Ltd, Welshpool, Powys, Wales
Printed and bound in Great Britain by Butler & Tanner, Frome

This book is dedicated to
Scott and Kate

ACKNOWLEDGMENTS

Welcome to the *Stamford Bridge Encyclopedia*, a work which, though not comprehensive, includes all those moments, players, memories, and characters which have made Chelsea the club it is today. The idea of the encyclopedia is not to supply in full a players' index, although I like to think those selected will provoke some form of memory, be it good or bad.

In recent times there have been a number of works covering the history of the club, these can become confusing and at times rather intimidating as one wades through season by season statistics and ephemeral data. This is where the *Stamford Bridge Encyclopedia* comes into its own, easy to digest and simple in its conception it is the book I always searched for as a youngster.

I hope you enjoy reading this work half as much as I have enjoyed researching and writing it. I have picked supporters' brains from all over the country, talking to the so-called 'experts' and seeking out those forgotten times and incidents which are worth recording. Chelsea is a big club, a big club with a big future. But for now I will deal only with the past recording the best of the first 90 years.

I would like to take this opportunity to thank many agencies and bodies for their assistance in this work. Sincere appreciation goes to: The Football Association, The Premier League, The Football League, The Association of Football Statisticians, Bill Campbell at Mainstream Publishing for the opportunity of putting it all into print, the staff of the British Newspaper Library, Colindale. Thanks go to Mike Capps of KAPPA Sport Pictures, Kettering, who can supply copies of those illustrations included in this work if required. To Mark Harrison for his timely reminders and influence upon the book. To Lesley, Paula, and Mark, my family who had to suffer my infernal ramblings about fact after fact during the research and writing. Finally, to all those Chelsea fans who proffered so much information and time; brilliant, each and every one of you.

Paul Harrison
Summer 1995

A

ALLEN, CECIL. Strong, athletic defender, Allen was robust in the tackle and cleared his lines well. He remained at the Bridge for a relatively short period, between 1935–1936 when he returned to his native Ireland and Cliftonville. He made one full Irish International appearance against England in 1936.

ALLEN, CLIVE. England International centre-forward with 5 caps. Clive Allen was a much experienced and well-travelled striker when he arrived at Chelsea in December 1991. His professional career began at another club, Queen's Park Rangers, for whom he signed professional terms in September 1978. An incredible transfer to Arsenal in June 1980 saw him appear on the Gunners' team photograph for the coming 1980/81 season. Without kicking a competitive ball for the club he was sold to Crystal Palace in August the same year! From there came a move to Tottenham, then a spell overseas with Bordeaux, followed by an uncharacteristic move North to Manchester before a move to Chelsea. Unable to hold down a regular first-team place, Allen was in and out of the side, but still managed to score 9 goals in a short Chelsea career of 22 games. Sold to yet another London side in April 1992, he now plays his football at West Ham United's Upton Park/Boleyn Ground.

ALLEN, LESLIE. Father of Clive, and a centre-forward of some note in his own right. An England U23 International, he signed professional terms with the Blues in September 1954 having previously played for Brigg Sports. A large and powerful forward, he would hustle and bustle defenders into making mistakes and was fully proficient at finishing moves.

Unfortunately he never really managed a long spell in the Chelsea side, but played 44 league games, scoring 11 goals, before being transferred to Tottenham Hotspur in an exchange deal with Johnny Brooks in December 1959. At White Hart Lane his career took off and honours followed. He tried his hand at club management with Queen's Park Rangers between 1967–1971 when he resigned. He later moved to Swindon Town in November 1972 but resigned in February 1974; Swindon were relegated at the end of that season. Honours as a player include; Football League Champions 1961, Division Three Champions 1967. FA Cup Winners 1961, Football League Cup Winners 1967, Division Two Runners-Up 1968.

ALLON, JOE. Blond-haired striker who generally failed to inspire whilst at Chelsea. Born in Gateshead he signed for Newcastle United in 1984 but was released by the Geordies in the 1987/88 season. Allon then moved to Swansea City, Hartlepool United, and Port Vale (on loan) before signing for Chelsea in the 1991/92 season. Sadly, although extremely enthusiastic he seems a player destined to excel only in lower league football.

ANDERTON, SYLVAN. Born in Reading, and brought to Chelsea in March 1959 by manager Ted Drake who knew his skills well enough from his own days at Elm Park. Anderton, a wing-half, was an industrious and dependable player who always played safe rather than gamble. There is nothing wrong with that, although it can be interpreted as lacking ambition. Certainly Anderton was not what one could call an enthusiastic or effervescent footballer. In layman's terms he was a worker bee, and quite happy to remain so. He moved to Queen's Park Rangers in January 1962 having made 82 appearances for Chelsea scoring 2 goals, he made just four league appearances for Rangers.

APPEARANCES. Ron 'Chopper' Harris made some 655 appearances between signing for the club as a professional in November 1961 and May 1980. A Chelsea club record which will take a lot of beating. Peter Houseman played in every competitive fixture of the 1969/70 season; a total of 54 games. He scored just 3 league goals during this run, but added a further 6 in the successful FA Cup run of that season, one of which was scored in the Wembley final against Leeds United. Ex-Chelsea player and manager, John Hollins stands joint seventh in the overall statistics for players who have made the most football league appearances. Hollins, alongside Alan Ball, has made 743 league appearances; 465 for Chelsea, 151 for Queen's Park Rangers, 127 for Arsenal, between 1964–1984.

ARGUE, JAMES. Inside-forward who was signed during the 1934/35 season from Birmingham City by manager Leslie Knighton. Argue proved a reliable acquisition. A tricky player, his strength on the ball and quick thinking ensured that he was a handful for any defence. Although his playing career was badly disrupted by the war years, Jimmy Argue returned to the Bridge in 1946, but found the competition for first-team places tough. He made just one appearance in the 1946/47 season and scored, before drifting out of Chelsea's side. Many fans still refer to 'Ginger' Argue to this very day, his hat-trick in the 5–5 draw with Bolton Wanderers during the 1937/38 season was an awe-inspiring display of his trickery and goal-grabbing skills.

ARIS SALONIKA. Chelsea's first-round opponents in the 1970/71 European Cup Winners Cup. The first leg took place in Salonika, Greece, on September 17 1990 and resulted in a 1–1 draw, with Ian Hutchinson scoring a vital away goal for the Blues. The second leg took place 13 days later on 30 September 1970. Chelsea were irresistible, and powered their way to a 5–1 victory with goals from Hollins 2, Hutchinson 2, and Hinton.

ARMSTRONG, KENNETH. A true Blue, Armstrong, a Yorkshireman, began his playing days with Bradford Rovers. He signed for Chelsea in December 1946 and never looked back. He made one full England International appearance and captained Chelsea. Armstrong genuinely enjoyed the game, was a strong intelligent right-half, and a magnificent motivator who led the club to a marvellous league Championship in the 1954/55 season. Armstrong ran and ran until he could run no more, and he fully expected those around him to do the same. His leadership often ensured that they did. He made 362 league appearances scoring 25 goals. He emigrated to New Zealand in May 1957 where he continued to play the game he loved so much, with Eastern Union, North Shore United, and Gisborne, as well as the New Zealand national squad. He was later elected as Chief Coach to the country's FA.

ATHLETIC CLUB. The London Athletic Club were the original tenants of the Stamford Bridge Stadium which was opened in April 1877. Formerly a market garden, the site was purchased by the Waddell brothers for just £2,599. The two brothers were something of entrepreneurs, and while their business sense was on this occasion to be applauded, they were far from shrewd. Just six years later they had fled the country leaving the Athletic Club with colossal debts. The club were, in effect, saved from extinction when a wealthy Athletic fan by the name of Stunt paid off the debts and took over the freehold of the ground building two small grandstands in the South West corner of the stadium. By 1902 Stunt had passed away. Then came a tug of war as to who would take over the ownership of the London Athletic Club Stadium. The Mears brothers won and set about building a stadium fit for football. The London Athletic Club were included in the new venture and remained within the stadium until 1912. Had it not been for the Mears brothers it is questionable as to whether there would now be a Chelsea FC or even a Stamford Bridge Stadium!

ATTENDANCES. The official highest attendance for a league fixture at Stamford Bridge stands at 82,905 against Arsenal in a Division 1 fixture on 12 October 1935. The game ended in a 1–1 draw. This is the second highest football league attendance of all time. The unofficial highest attendance took place in November 1945. Dinamo Moscow Football Club were playing a four match tour of Britain, with Chelsea lined up as their first opponents. It is a known fact that some 74,496 persons were officially within the stadium, however many more thousands entered by unofficial means. Most authorities agree that somewhere in the region of 90,000 were present to see Chelsea and Dinamo play out a thrilling 3–3 draw. As one of the bigger football clubs in England, Chelsea FC will always be an attraction, and so their presence in certain towns and cities has in the past ensured the host club their highest ever attendance figure; Newcastle United, 68,386, on 3 September 1930 for a Division 1 fixture, Chester City, 20,500 at the Sealand Road ground on 16 January 1952, for an FA Cup 3rd round replay, Cambridge United, 14,000 for a friendly fixture on 1 May 1970.

The highest average attendance figure for an entire season stands at an incredible 48,260 during the Championship-winning season of 1954/55. The lowest average attendance is, by comparison, a miserable 12,672 for the 1982/83 season. Although virtually impossible to be precise, most experts and football statisticians confirm that overall, since their formation in 1905, Chelsea have been the sixth best supported club in England. However, seasonal attendances fluctuate enough for this to change almost weekly dependent on the respective clubs' fortunes.

ATVIDABERG. Opponents in the 1971/72 European Cup Winners Cup, when they faced Chelsea in the second round. After a 0–0 draw in Sweden, Chelsea must have fancied their chances back at Stamford Bridge before a partisan 28,071 crowd. There the dream ends and the nightmare begins, for the Swedish side snatched a 1–1 draw to go through on the away goals rule! The Blues goal was scored by Alan Hudson.

AYLOTT, TREVOR. Progressed through the junior ranks of the club to sign professional terms in July 1976. Trevor Aylott was a tall, muscular striker who knew little else but the art of scoring goals, a knack which has yielded its rewards for him and his many clubs during his varied career in the game. He scored on his full league debut, a sweet, headed goal via Charlie Cookes' precise cross against Bristol City on 29 October 1977. He once again scored the match-winner against Nottingham Forest the following Saturday. Unfortunately, as is so often the case, the striker then went through a barren period in front of goal, which was sufficient to see him virtually fade from the side. After a further 27 appearances without a first-team goal, the writing was on the wall. Aylott was sold to Barnsley in November where he bagged 26 goals in 96 appearances. He later played for Millwall, Luton Town, Crystal Palace, Barnsley (on loan), AFC Bournemouth, Birmingham City, Oxford United and Gillingham.

B

BAIN, JAMES. Winger signed shortly after the Second World War who had impressed scouts monitoring his talents whilst at Gillingham pre-1939. Bain played out just one season at the Bridge, that being 1946/47 when he made 9 league appearances and scored one goal before being sold to Swindon Town in May 1947.

BAKER, BENJAMIN. Goalkeeper whose ability should never be underestimated. Benjamin Howard Baker was born in Liverpool, in 1892. His playing days commenced with Marlborough Old Boys, then came a spell with the Northern Nomads, and a short time in the Blackburn Rover reserves. Baker even had a trial with England amateurs as centre-half! It was Everton who first introduced him to competitive football before Chelsea signed him in the early Twenties. Baker was a real personality and an outstanding sportsman. For a while he held the British High Jump record, clearing 5' 6" at a meeting held at Huddersfield on 5 June 1921. He made 2 appearances, for the England full International side, in 1921 v Belgium, and, whilst with Chelsea, in 1926 v Northern Ireland. There were a further 10 amateur International appearances for his country. Upon leaving Stamford Bridge he had a spell with Oldham

Athletic. He was an exceptional goalkeeper, with a huge kick and superb reactions.

BAKER, GERRY. The brother of the outstanding striker Joe Baker. Gerry struggled to make the grade at Chelsea and, after being signed in June 1955, he never broke into the first team and was transferred to Manchester City in November 1960.

BALDWIN, THOMAS. One of the Chelsea greats, Tommy Baldwin was lethal in the air and powerful on the ground. A Geordie, his first professional club was, in fact, Arsenal. He moved to Chelsea in September 1966 and so commenced a fine relationship between player and club. Baldwin was a grafter, committing himself to every tackle, but would often lose this enthusiasm part way through a game causing frustration among fans and club management alike. Injury prone, he found himself out of the side with alarming frequency, and this seriously hampered his football career in general. Eventually, after one injury he was displaced from the team by Ian Hutchinson, and that was basically the end of his Chelsea career. Brief loan spells with Millwall and Manchester United during the 1974/75 season failed to yield a permanent move and Baldwin was eventually freed by the club and drifted into the non-league circuit, turning out for Gravesend and Northfleet. Brentford offered a lifeline in 1977 when he was given non-contract terms, but again this proved inconclusive.

BAMBRICK, JOSEPH. Forward signed from Linfield, Ireland, in the 1934/35 season. Bambrick was an adaptable player, good with either foot and a neat distributor of the ball. His strength was forcing his way past defenders on the edge of the penalty area.

On 16 March 1935 he scored four goals at Stamford Bridge in a first division fixture against Leeds United, which Chelsea won 7–1. He gained 4 full International caps for Northern Ireland whilst at Stamford Bridge; 1935 v Wales, 1936 v England and Scotland, and 1938 v Wales.

BARNARD, DARREN. Defender, Barnard looks to be yet another useful proposition in the Blues line-up. He is cool, calm and collected on the ball and has already scored 2 goals for the first team in just a handful of appearances. With a little more confidence he should be able to stake a regular claim for first-team football.

BARNESS, ANTHONY. Promising defender who has emerged during the last few seasons. To date he has made in the region of 20-plus appearances and were it not for the presence of Steve Clarke he would surely have made a first-team place his own. Signed for Charlton first in September 1992.

BASON, BRIAN. Midfielder and England School International, Bason signed professional for the club in September 1972. His potential was never truly realised as he made just 18 league appearances, scoring one goal between 1972–1976. He was sold to Plymouth Argyle and later played for Crystal Palace, Portsmouth and Reading.

BELLETT, WALLY. Full-back and yet another England Youth International, Wally was 21 years of age when signed by Chelsea from Barking FC in September 1954. Somewhat inconsistent he made just 35 League appearances, scoring one goal between 1955–1958 when he was sold to Plymouth Argyle. Spent the rest of his career in the lower leagues with, Chelmsford City, Orient, Chester City, Wrexham and Tranmere Rovers.

BENTLEY, ROY. Roy's professional career began at Bristol Rovers in 1941 where his talent as a centre-half was sufficient for North East giants Newcastle United to spend £8,500 on him. Bentley proved his worth and bagged 21 league goals in 48 outings. Chelsea paid £12,500 for his services in January 1948 and tried him out as a centre-forward. It worked, Bentley was phenomenal in front of goal and scored 128 league goals in 324 appearances for the Blues between 1948 and September 1956 when he was sold to Fulham. An England International he was honoured with

12 England full International appearances in which he scored 9 goals. Each of his International appearances were made whilst on Chelsea's books. He later appeared for Queen's Park Rangers, and managed Swansea and Reading.

BERRY, PAUL. Centre-half who seemed to have a marvellous career ahead of him when spotted playing local football. He progressed through the juniors to sign professional in April 1953. Sadly, he never made it, with only 3 league appearances in the 1956/57 season, he was another prospect lost to the game through an abundance of quality elsewhere within the squad.

BETTERIDGE, WALTER. This slightly-built right-back possessed so much talent that he virtually maintained a first-team place for almost 11 years. First appearing in the 1910/11 season, he was a marvellous club servant with a useful turn of pace and an ability to recover defensive errors. Few players of his era were afforded as much respect as Betteridge, and he played his final game for the club in the 1921/22 season.

BILLINGTON, HUGH. Centre-forward with a huge desire to win and succeed. Born in Bedfordshire he was signed by Luton Town after impressing with local side Waterlows. He scored 35 league goals in 60 games for the Hatters before transferring to Chelsea in March 1948. Billington was a reasonable striker, certainly his goal tally is as impressive as any other top forward of the era; 28 league goals from 83 games between 1948–1950. His age, however, held him up for, by the time he arrived at Stamford Bridge, he was 32 and, some claimed, past his best.

BIRCHENALL, ALAN. Blond-haired cult-hero striker Birch could be brilliant or awful. Thankfully for much of his Chelsea career he tended to be brilliant. His playing days began with Sheffield United before Chelsea signed him in November 1967. A striking partner to Peter Osgood he possessed a powerful shot and was a master at holding the ball for others to feed off. He made four England U23

THE STAMFORD BRIDGE ENCYCLOPEDIA

International appearances but never received a call for full International duty. With his striking appearance he had many fan clubs and seemed to relish the attention the professional game offered him. In 74 league appearances he scored 20 goals before being sold to Crystal Palace. He then moved to Leicester City where he matured into one of the country's finest strikers. He later appeared for Notts County, Memphis Rogues, Blackburn Rovers, Luton Town and Hereford United. He is now employed by Leicester City in an administrative capacity. He is still a real character, and his remarks over the Leicester tannoy system criticising the match referee against Coventry City show his obvious love for the game. A well-respected man, and a star in his own right.

BIRRELL, WILLIAM. Chelsea manager, May 1939–May 1952. Birrell's playing career took in Inverkeithing United, Raith Rovers and Middlesbrough before he turned to management in 1927 with a return to Scottish club side, Raith Rovers. Birrell was a genuinely nice man who impressed many with his innovative style at Raith and it was no surprise when he returned to the English game as manager of Bournemouth and Boscombe Athletic in 1930. Then followed a 4-year spell as manager/secretary of Queen's Park Rangers between 1935–1939. Birrell arrived at Stamford Bridge in the May of 1939 with the club struggling to maintain any consistency in the 1st Division. After the war he introduced what has been classed as one of the greatest youth policy schemes in football, which has continued to prosper ever since. Chelsea appeared in two wartime Cup Finals under his guidance as well as reaching the semi-final of the competition in 1950 and 1952. He left the club in May 1952; a well-respected manager whose foresight was far greater than many of his contemporaries.

BISHOP, SYDNEY. Stepney-born wing-half, the distinguished-sounding Sydney Macdonald Bishop had a varied and interesting football career, crowned by 4 full International appearances for England in 1927. His career allowed him to grace the colours of Crystal Palace, West

Ham United and Leicester City before a final move to Stamford Bridge in June 1928. Unfortunately this time at Chelsea was less than impressive, and he never matched the quality of his performances during his West Ham days. A master of ball control, he gave the impression of being relaxed with the ball at his feet. He also had the ability to outjump the tallest of opponents, with a powerful header to match. He retired from playing whilst at Chelsea at the end of the 1932/33 season.

BLANCHFLOWER, DENNIO. Danny Blanchflower was a well-respected and outstanding footballer of his generation. A right-half, he was the ultimate reader of the game, blessed with the skill to tear defences open with one pass. He was one of the few players who was able to control the pace and style of a game. His best days as a player were at Tottenham Hotspur.

Blanchflower retired as a player in 1963 and took up the manager's position for Northern Ireland in June 1976. He was something of a dinosaur in the game of the 1970s, and while his knowledge was undeniably brilliant this was not sufficient for the modern game. It came as some surprise when he was announced as manager of Chelsea in December 1978. The club saw Blanchflower as a high-profile character and personality who would attract the crowds and quality players. He did neither, and was honest enough to admit defeat, modern methods and styles were too much for him to cope with and he resigned as Chelsea manager after just nine months in charge; a sad end to an illustrious and proud career.

BLOCK, MICHAEL. Right-winger signed from the juniors in February 1957. Block was a typical speedy and artistic winger, if often temperamental and inconsistent. He made 37 league appearances scoring 6 goals, before a move to Brentford in January 1962.

BLUNSTONE, FRANK. It has often been said that footballers require skill, stamina and courage. Frank Blunstone possessed the lot, he was an outstanding talent, a left-winger of such precocious quality that he was always going to be a success. His playing career started with Crewe Alexandra before he joined Chelsea in 1953. At the Bridge he went on to make 347 appearances and score 54 goals before injury forced him to retire, but club loyalty provided him with an opportunity to join the coaching staff, which he did in October 1954.

Twice during his career he suffered leg breaks, one of which kept him out for the whole of the 1957/58 season. An integral part of the Chelsea machine which won the 1955 Football League Championship, the sight of Blunstone hurtling down the left wing, his feet dancing, was a marvel to behold. After some 16 years at the club he eventually took over as manager of Brentford FC. His career thereafter took him onto the coaching staff of such clubs as Manchester United, Derby County, Aris Salonika and Sheffield Wednesday. He was a highly-respected figure in the game.

BOLLAND, GORDON. Another player who failed to impress at Chelsea but progressed to be a fine player elsewhere. Bolland was a product of the junior side, a striker who seemed full of confidence whilst playing local league soccer. He signed professional terms for the Blues in August 1960 but was, frankly, uninspiring. He made just 2 league appearances in 1961 before a transfer to Orient, then Norwich, Charlton, and finally Millwall where he turned in some outstanding performances.

BONETTI, PETER. The Cat. What can one say about this acrobatic, slimline keeper? Bonetti was an outstanding goalkeeper of his time, some believe the best in the world, although his critics will recall the England – West Germany World Cup game in 1970 when he seemed glued to his line when the German Muller came anywhere near goal. But one poor game in an outstanding career can be no indictment upon his undoubted quality. Bonetti seemed to pull off the impossible in every game in which he featured, with flying leaps to the left or right, at times he seemed unbeatable. Chelsea was his sole professional club, after he joined them as a junior, signing in May 1959. He made his Chelsea debut at the tender age of 17, and clocked up some 600 league appearances. He won many honours, including the FA Cup, and European Cup Winners Cup medals, as well as 7 full International appearances for England, which would have been many more had it not been for the presence of one Gordon Banks in the England goalkeeper's jersey. His worst memory is probably that of a league cup tie at Carlisle United's Brunton Park in 1970, when he had a stone thrown at him, which struck his head and knocked him unconscious. Despite this he got up and played on, only to lose 1–0. Bonetti made no great fuss about the matter and maintained his dignity, something he continued to do throughout his excellent career.

BOROTA, PETAR. Yugoslavian International goalkeeper signed from Partizan Belgrade in March 1979. Borota was an effective and well-liked shot-stopper. The fans worshipped him. Something of an 'eccentric', he would commit the most ridiculous acts, charging out of his own penalty area to break down attacks which were hardly penetrating or dangerous. Borota won Chelsea fans' Player of the Year Awards during his two-year spell with the club and broke Peter Bonetti's record of consecutive 'clean sheets' when he kept 16 in the 1980/81 season. Moved to Brentford in 1981.

BOWER, ALFRED. England International full-back who was astute with either foot and often played in either full-back position. Born in Kent in November 1895, he first signed for Old Carthusians before arriving at Stamford Bridge. He found life difficult at Chelsea and his stay was but a brief one before he moved on to Casuals, then Corinthians in 1923 where he gained all of his 5 International caps. He also captained the club. For whatever reason he never settled at Chelsea and was undoubtedly a quality player lost by the club.

BOWIE, JAMES. A Scot, Jim Bowie was born in Aberdeen in 1924. Signed from Park Vale after the Second World War he made a total of 76 league appearances for Chelsea and scored 18 goals before being transferred to Fulham in January 1951. Bowie later played for Brentford and Watford.

BOYD, THOMAS. Scottish International defender who was signed from Motherwell in June 1991. Boyd had excelled in the Scottish game proving himself a hard and workmanlike defender. He was signed as a replacement for Tony Dorigo, but failed to achieve anything like the form of his predecessor. He made 31 appearances in his eight-month stay at the Bridge before being used as bait in an exchange deal with Glasgow Celtic for Tony Cascarino.

BOYLE, JOHN. A marvellous club servant, John Boyle arrived via the junior set up in 1964. A wing-half, his strong physical approach to the game was cleverly supplemented by a neat touch and a fine passing ability. A difficult player to dispossess he went on to make over 250 first-team appearances for Chelsea winning honours in the 1965 League Cup final and in the European Cup Winners Cup. Few would deny his enthusiasm for the game. Boyle was a true professional. Injuries tended to keep him out of a regular first-team place but he always acquitted himself well. By 1973 his Chelsea career seemed over with the emergence of younger, fresher talent. Boyle went on loan to Brighton and Hove Albion but never signed for the club and was eventually released to Orient in December of that year. He later played football in the USA.

BRABROOK, PETER. Another product of the Chelsea juniors who signed professional terms in March 1955. Brabrook was as quick a footballer as you will ever see. Many defenders were left in his wake as the head went down and off he went. He was one of the few players who could cross accurate balls with either foot. He made 3 International appearances for England whilst at Chelsea. Between 1954–1961 he made over 250 appearances for Chelsea netting well over 50 goals. He was sold to West Ham in October 1961.

BRADSHAW, JOSEPH. A rather ordinary winger who arrived at the club from near neighbours Fulham in May 1909. Bradshaw failed to make any impact at the Bridge and was transferred to Queen's Park Rangers within twelve months. He later tried his hand at club management with Southend United, Swansea Town, Fulham and Bristol City.

BRAWN, WILLIAM. Huge figure of a centre-forward, standing at 6' 2" and weighing in at 15 plus stones, Brawn was an apt name for this man. He joined Chelsea in 1907 after a spell with Middlesbrough. His career had been somewhat illustrious, as he turned out for Northampton Town, Sheffield United, and Aston Villa prior to Boro; he was a member of the Villa FA Cup-winning squad of 1905 and an England International. Brawn was a robust figure who was well liked during a 4-year stay at Stamford Bridge. He was sold to Brentford in 1911.

BRAZIL. It was Chelsea Football Club who brought to the attention of an unsuspecting football world the emergence of Brazil as a force within the world game. Prior to the Blues' tour of 1930 the Brazilians had never been classed as quality opposition for any International side. How the perception has changed in the years since then.

BRIDGES, BARRY. Hard, solid and determined centre-forward who first joined Chelsea as a junior in July 1956 signing professional in May 1958. He represented England Youth at International level. Barry Bridges was a real favourite of the Stamford Bridge crowd. His bustling and hustling in and around the opponent's penalty area won the occasional penalty kick or created an opportunity for a shot at goal. A Football League Cup winner with the club in 1965 he was always an achiever. He made 293 appearances for the club, scoring 93 goals before being sold to Birmingham in May 1966. He later played for Queen's Park Rangers, Millwall, and Brighton and Hove Albion and made 4 full International appearances for England.

BRITTON, IAN. Diminutive midfielder who was a 90-minute player, committed to every tackle, shot, pass, or move. Britton carved out a fine Chelsea career for himself between 1972–1981 when he chalked up some 279 appearances banging in 34 goals into the bargain. Sadly, as his career progressed and Chelsea won promotion to the first division, he seemed to hide in games, and would not gamble with his shots or passes. In essence he was too safe, his game was easily read by the opposition. He moved to Dundee United in 1981 after his loss of confidence and returned to the English game in December 1983 with Blackpool. Britton, despite his latter years at the club, was a real terrier and a true Blue.

BROOKS, JOHN. Clever inside-forward whose playing days began with Reading FC in April 1949. His trickery on the ball interested Tottenham who signed him in February 1953. England International recognition beckoned and he went on to gain three full caps for his country. Brooks signed for Chelsea in December 1959 but was hardly the enthusiastic star he had been when making his name earlier in his career. Saying that, he did make 46 league appearances and scored 6 goals but seemed to lack the flair which Chelsea had hoped would spark their side. In September 1961 he was sold to Brentford and later moved on to Crystal Palace.

BROWN, WILLIAM. If commitment was to be rewarded, Bill Brown would have won all sorts of prizes. Born in County Durham he somehow slipped through the Newcastle United scouting network and found himself playing for West Ham United in 1922. He was part of the side which lost to Bolton Wanderers in the 1923 FA Cup final. His ball control was an outstanding feature of his game. The lure of Chelsea proved too great for him to resist as he signed for the club in February 1924. He gained a solitary full England International cap in 1924 whilst with the Hammers and moved to Fulham in 1929.

BUCHANAN, PETER. Inside-forward born in Glasgow in 1915. Peter Buchanan was signed by Chelsea from Wishaw

Juniors. He progressed to International recognition, making his solitary appearance for Scotland against Czechoslovakia in 1938. He was a real flier, with the ball at his feet he would weave in and out of defences with often incredible skill. Sadly, all too often he would deceive himself and lose control of the ball. However, his ability could turn up trumps and win matches. After the war he signed for Fulham and later played for Brentford.

BURGESS, HARRY. Born in Cheshire in 1904, the well-built, solid forward and artful goalscorer Burgess appeared for Stockport County and Sandbach Ramblers (loan), before a big move to Sheffield Wednesday in June 1929. Whilst at Hillsborough he won a Football League Championship medal in 1930, which was followed by further recognition at International level; 4 full caps for England during 1931.

He came to Chelsea in March 1935 and continued to score goals, though sadly his career was decimated by the war years and he retired from the game whilst on Chelsea's books during hostilities. Burgess was indeed a great talent.

BURLEY, CRAIG. Strong, athletic Scottish striker, Craig Burley has emerged as a bright young talent since making his first-team debut for the club at Tottenham Hotspur in December 1992. Since then he has scored several goals and has earned the respect of his playing colleagues and fans alike. One of his goals came during the 94/95 season in a 2–2 draw at Ipswich, a critical equaliser which may well prove costly to Ipswich who are facing relegation. Nothing unusual about that you may feel, but Craig is actually the nephew of Ipswich manager George Burley!

BUMSTEAD, JOHN. A solid and reliable midfielder, John Bumstead signed for Chelsea in March 1978 and proved to be one of the most consistent players at the club during his 13 year stay. Having made some 379 appearances and scored 44 goals, his role in the side should never be underestimated.

Injuries followed and generally spoiled his game. Such hard-working players all too often find themselves sidelined

Craig Burley

through such niggling incidents. Bumstead, to his credit, bounced back every time. He was, at the age of 33, given a free transfer to Charlton Athletic who profited from his vast experience and quality play. Sadly he was forced to retire from the game when a back injury proved too painful for him to continue in 1993.

BUSBY, Sir MATTHEW, CBE. Yes, no printing error, Sir Matt Busby did don the famous all-blue shirt of Chelsea FC.

27

He made three guest appearances for the club during the Second World War!

C

CALDERHEAD, DAVID (Junior). Centre-half who lacked the composure to prove himself a worthy capture. Born in Scotland, it was perhaps no coincidence that at the time he made his Chelsea outings, his father was in charge of first-team affairs. Calderhead signed from Lincoln City in September 1907 before being released to Motherwell in April 1914.

CALDERHEAD, DAVID (Senior). An unsung hero, Dave Calderhead was remarkably loyal to Chelsea FC, remaining at the club for some 26 years in a managerial role. His playing career began in Scottish junior football before a move to Queen of the South Wanderers in 1881. Eight years later, a Scottish International, he moved to Notts County, then spent 7 years as secretary/manager of Lincoln City. Joined Chelsea as manager in July 1907 and began to lay the foundations for the future of the club. A quiet, unassuming character he went about his job in a gentlemanly manner. On the field Chelsea were somewhat inconsistent, however they did reach the FA Cup final in 1915, only to lose to Sheffield United, in what was known as 'The Khaki Final'. Retired from the game at the end of the 1932/33 season, when the club won just fourteen games all season, and were just two points from the bottom of the 1st Division.

CAMERON, JOCK. Sturdy, reliable full-back who was an arrogant ball winner. Cameron's ability to dispossess and turn the play around earned him great praise from the press and football public at the end of the 20th-century's first decade.

CAMPBELL, BOBBY. Team manager May 1988 – May 1991. As a player, Bobby Campbell had a fairly undistinguished career after a promising start. A product of Liverpool's outstanding youth structure he signed professional at Anfield in May 1954, making his first-team debut in 1958. A wing-half, he represented the England Youth as an adolescent but never fulfilled the expectations of those coaching him. Twenty-four league games and 2 goals later he signed for Wigan Athletic before returning to the professional game with Portsmouth in May 1961. His career eventually saw him ending up at the Recreation Ground, Aldershot. After retiring from playing he took on a number of coaching roles with Pompey, Queen's Park Rangers, Arsenal and Fulham before becoming manager at Craven Cottage in 1976. He then went on a merry-go-round of assistant-manager/manager positions with Aldershot, Portsmouth and Arsenal before returning to Loftus Road (QPR) as reserve-team coach. He came to Stamford Bridge in a promoted role; first-team coach in March 1988. He took over as manager when John Hollins departed in May of the same year. Campbell took the team to the 2nd Division championship in the 1988/89 season, and the following season the side topped the then 1st Division for a short time, finally finishing in fifth position. With big money signings arriving at the Bridge the 1990/91 season looked promising, but apart from a Rumbelows Cup semi-final appearance, and defeat at the hands of Sheffield Wednesday little went right for the club and so Campbell was replaced as team manager in May 1991.

CAMPBELL, ROBERT. Glaswegian and a sensational outside-right who progressed to make 5 Scottish full

Bobby Campbell

International appearances, 3 with Chelsea and 2 with his previous club side, Falkirk. Campbell arrived at Stamford Bridge in May 1947 and went on to make a total of 188 league appearances, scoring 36 goals into the bargain. Few wingers have been so devastating in Chelsea blue. Campbell's flair and ingenuity were an outstanding feature of many games in which he featured. In August 1954 at the age of 32 he was sold to Reading where he went on to make a further 95 league appearances until he left Elm Park in 1957. A remarkable winger who would not look out of place in today's game.

CANOVILLE, PAUL. Signed from Hillingdon Borough in December 1981, Canoville was an athletic and well-balanced forward. He made a total of 67 appearances for the Blues, scoring 15 goals. His commitment was at times open to debate, as he would fail to make any impact in some games, then in others he would give everything. No more so than in the epic Milk Cup tie against Sheffield Wednesday in 1985 when he inspired Chelsea to a remarkable fight back from 3–0 down to a 4–4 draw, in which he bagged two goals. In August 1986 he moved from Chelsea to Reading where injury all but forced him to quit the game in 1988. Canoville was a frustrating sort of player who, on his day was unstoppable, but who on other days simply didn't seem to want to know.

CASCARINO, ANTHONY. Tony Cascarino was a vastly-experienced and prolific goalscorer when he arrived at Chelsea in February 1992, with Tommy Boyd moving to Celtic as part of the exchange deal. Tall and lean his great strength is in the air, although he also boasts a powerful shot. Cascarino was a rough and rugged-style centre-forward, although he should not be classed as unqualified. His skill and adaptability made him a winner. He initially made a name for himself as a striker with Gillingham, then came a move to Millwall, Aston Villa and Glasgow Celtic. Cascarino is currently scoring goals for Wimbledon, and is still a real handful for any defence.

CASEY, LEN. London-born wing-half, Casey signed for Chelsea from Leyton in February 1954. A solid, well-built player he was robust in the tackle and was given a 'hard man' tag. Off the field, as is generally the case, he was a quiet, polite man who wore a permanent smile on his face. He made just 38 appearances before being transferred to Plymouth Argyle in December 1958.

CHEYNE, ALEX. Big money signing from Aberdeen at the beginning of the 1930/31 season, Cheyne then cost £6,000, money which although regarded as well spent, was not really fortuitous on the playing front. Cheyne often

Tony Cascarino

flattered to deceive and although a player of undoubted talent he never really settled in at the Bridge. A member of the team with some outstanding talents, such as Gallacher, Wilson and Crawford. Alongside these stars he was unfortunately a rather ordinary player.

CHIVERS, GARY. Apprentice who signed professional in August 1978, Gary Chivers was one of those footballers who one felt needed a kick up the backside to get him going. He gave the impression of strolling through each game, unflustered and almost nonchalant. His skill factor was undeniable, his passing and reading of the game were impeccable, yet he seemed to lack the self belief that he was good enough. One hundred and forty three games and just 4 goals later he was sold to Swansea City in August 1983 and lasted just ten months there before he signed for Queen's Park Rangers in February 1984. He later moved to Watford then Brighton and Hove Albion.

CLARKE, STEVE. A fast and furious right-back, Steve Clarke enjoys nothing more than a speedy forward run up the right touchline, before cutting inside to have a serious crack at goal. Signed from Scottish side St Mirren, he has been a revelation in the Chelsea side of recent seasons.

Dependable and solid, his no-nonsense style of play has earned him much praise throughout the British game. Already a Scottish full International, more caps and honours seem certain for this defender.

CLISS, DAVID. Enfield-born, and signed through the Chelsea juniors, David Cliss was a slightly-built and diminutive inside-forward whose first touch was outstanding. Despite such talent, Cliss never made it, his performances, although good, were spoiled by his lightweight approach making him easily dispossessed. After 24 games and one goal he finally drifted into the non-league game in 1961.

CLOSE. Few seasons will be as close at the final whistle as that of the 1962/63 season. Chelsea went to Roker Park, Sunderland on Wednesday 28 May 1963 in a vital 2nd Division fixture with both clubs placed in second and third positions respectively, so both had an excellent chance of promotion. Chelsea won the game 1–0 by virtue of a Tommy Harmer goal in the 26th minute, Harmer's first goal of the season! Despite the victory, Chelsea, although handily placed, had a far inferior goal difference to Sunderland and Stoke City, so it was down to the last match of the season. In an amazing game, Chelsea thrashed Portsmouth 7–0 at Stamford Bridge with Bobby Tambling helping himself to four goals. The result ensured that the Blues pipped Sunderland for second spot in the division and won promotion by 1.928 of a goal.

COCK, 'JACK', JOHN. Signed from trouble-torn Huddersfield Town in October 1919 for a fee of £2,500, Jack Cock was, by anyone's standards, a bargain buy. Fast, athletic player whose build meant that not only could he hold off challenges, but he also had the agility to dive, stoop, or leap to head home goals. Cock was everything one could dream of in a centre-forward. An England International, he made 2 appearances for his country in 1920. Sadly, Cock found his talents a great burden as defenders would stick to him like glue, he was identified as a target for rough-and-ready tackles. Slowly but surely his game and goals diminished, until 1923, when Chelsea felt it in the interests of both player and club to sell him. Thus, in January of that same year, he moved to Merseyside. He later appeared for Plymouth Argyle, Millwall, Folkestone, and Walton FC in October 1932. Later managed Millwall from November 1944 – August 1948 before retiring from the game completely. Cock was very much a quality player whose ability was his own downfall as his temperament and resilience failed to lift him above the basic rudiments of the game.

COLLINS, MICHAEL. Goalkeeper from Middlesbrough who was signed from non-league football, Redcar, in November 1951. Sadly the move was not a successful one for either Collins or the club, he made just one appearance for the club spending the rest of his time in the reserves. Not a hugely effective keeper, he was sold to Watford in July 1957.

COMPTON, JOHN. Full-back, from the Chelsea juniors, Compton signed professional in February 1955 but struggled to make any real impression upon the successful squad of the mid-Fifties. He made just 12 league appearances before moving on to Ipswich Town where his career prospered and he made well over 100 appearances for the Suffolk club. He later played for Bournemouth.

COOKE, CHARLES. Scottish International and a master of ball control, Charlie Cooke was a great crowd favourite at Stamford Bridge. He was an entertainer who could play as well in midfield as he could on the wing. Signed from Dundee in April 1966, he went on to serve Chelsea during two different spells making a total of 360 appearances and netting 30 goals. His weaving, almost magical dribbling skills guaranteed him honours, as a European Cup Winner in 1970/71, and an FA Cup winner in the 1969/70 season. Such artistic talents generally have some subtle flaw to their game, and Cooke was no different; so much talent, so much experience, yet all too often, too little application. He was sold to Crystal Palace in October 1972 in the hope that the move could rejuvenate his enthusiasm; it did, and Chelsea duly re-signed him in January 1974. He eventually succumbed to the promise of greater things in the USA where he played soccer as opposed to football, for Los Angeles Aztecs, Memphis Rogues and California Surf. The glitter and razzmatazz of the USA quickly diminished into a fallen dream, but even so, those who witnessed the fine skills of Charlie Cooke in full flight knew they had seen a real footballer, a real football idol.

COPELAND, DAVID. Signed from Tottenham Hotspur in May 1905, Copeland was a slight, fleet-footed player who operated on the left wing. He was signed by the club prior to their admission to the football league. It is without doubt that signings of such great quality enhanced Chelsea's chance of election to the league. He scored two goals in the club's first competitive home fixture at Stamford Bridge on 11 September 1905 when Hull City were succinctly despatched 5–1.

CORTHINE, PETER. Born in arch-rival territory, Highbury, North London, Peter Corthine was a striker who signed from Leytonstone in December 1957. A player who always seemed a temporary fixture in the Chelsea ranks, he made just 2 league appearances in 1959 without scoring and was duly transferred to Southend United in March 1960. Corthine proved to be a good signing for the Shrimpers, scoring on his debut in a 1–1 draw at Somerton Park in a league fixture against Newport County. He later moved into the non-league game turning out for Chelmsford City.

CRAIG, ALLAN. Signed from Motherwell in January 1933, Craig was a fine defender who was swopped from a wing-half position to that of a central defender. He earned 3 full Scottish International appearances whilst with Motherwell against Norway, Holland and England.

CRAWFORD, JOHN. Born in South Shields, this tricky winger's career began with Jarrow Celtic, before progressing to Palmers FC (Jarrow), then Hull City in March 1920. Crawford was a master of the crossed ball, on the run or from the dead-ball situation. His pin-point accurate crossing was a real threat to the best of defences. He signed for the Blues in May 1923 where he remained for some 11 years, and gained England full International recognition in 1931. Crawford was one of the few footballers who could operate from either wing. Later he signed for Queen's Park Rangers, for whom he was to become first-team coach in 1937.

CROAL, JAMES. Left-winger signed from Scottish club side, Falkirk in 1914. Croal scored many important goals in his time with the Blues, none more so than the one he netted against an on-form Everton in the FA Cup semi-final at Villa Park in 1915. Chelsea went on to defeat the Toffeemen 2–0 in that same semi. Interestingly, Croal also scored a semi-final goal the following season, in a 3–1 defeat against Aston Villa.

CROWTHER, STAN. Talented wing-half who was signed from Manchester United in December 1958 having previously impressed during his time at Aston Villa. Crowther was a tough-tackling player whose enthusiasm to get things going often led to the odd misdirected pass. An England U23 International he moved to Brighton and Hove Albion in March 1961. Crowther became the first man to appear in the FA Cup for different clubs in the same year, 1957/58. Today he would, of course, have been 'Cup-tied'.

CUP FINALS. Chelsea have appeared in 7 major Cup finals, these do not include Zenith Data or Full Members competitions. To date they have been successful on 3 occasions, winning the FA Cup in 1970, Football League Cup in 1965, and the European Cup Winners Cup in 1971. Team line-ups and dates of these finals are as follows:

1915 FA Cup Final
24 April v Sheffield United (Old Trafford) 0–3
Chelsea team: Molyneux, Bettridge, Harrow, Taylor, Logan, Walker, Ford, Halse, Thomson, Croal, McNeil.

1965 Football League Cup
First leg; 15 March v Leicester (Stamford Bridge) 3–2
Second leg; 5 April v Leicester (Filbert Street) 0–0
Chelsea won on aggregate 3–2
Chelsea team: Bonetti, Hinton, R. Harris, Hollins, Young, Boyle, Murray, Graham, McCreadie, Venables, Tambling.
Scorers: Tambling, Venables (pen) and McCreadie.

1967 FA Cup Final
20 May 1967 v Tottenham Hotspur (Wembley) 1–2
Chelsea team: Bonetti, A. Harris, McCreadie, Hollins, Hinton, R. Harris, Cooke, Baldwin, Hateley, Tambling, Boyle.
Scorer: Tambling.

1970 FA Cup Final
11 April v Leeds United (Wembley) 2–2
Chelsea team: Bonetti, Webb, McCreadie, Hollins, Dempsey, R. Harris, Baldwin, Houseman, Osgood, Hutchinson, Cooke, Sub. Hinton.
Scorers: Houseman, Hutchinson.

1970 FA Cup Final Replay
29 April v Leeds United (Old Trafford) 2–1
Chelsea team as above.
Scorers: Osgood, Webb.

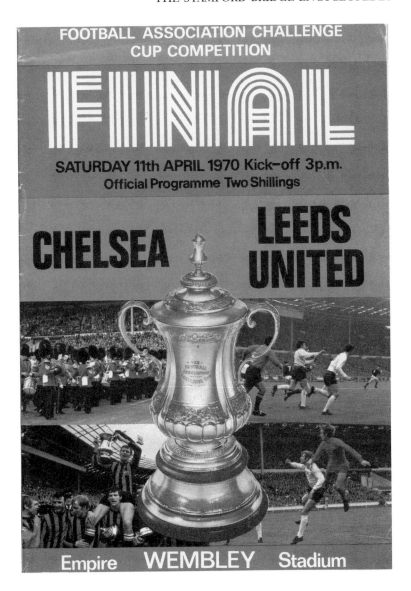

1971 European Cup Winners Cup
19 May v Real Madrid (Athens) 1–1
Chelsea team: Bonetti, Boyle, R. Harris, Cooke, Dempsey,
Webb, Weller, Baldwin, Osgood, Hudson, Houseman, Sub.
Smethurst.
Scorer: Osgood.

1971 European Cup Winners Cup Replay
21 May v Real Madrid (Athens) 2–1
Chelsea team as above.
Scorers: Dempsey, Osgood.

1975 Football League Cup
4 March v Stoke City (Wembley) 1–2
Chelsea team: Bonetti, Mulligan, R. Harris, Hollins, Dempsey, Webb, Cooke, Garland, Osgood, Hudson, Houseman, Sub. Baldwin.
Scorer: Osgood.

1994 FA Cup Final
14 May v Manchester United (Wembley) 0–4
Chelsea team: Kharin, Clarke, Johnson, Kjeldbjerg, Sinclair, Burley, Newton, Spencer, Peacock, Stein, Wise, Subs. Cascarino, Hoddle.

CURIOSITY. Tom Priestley, an inside-forward who starred for the club in the 1930s always wore a rugby scrum-cap when playing. This was due to a childhood illness which caused him to lose his hair. Nothing to do with vanity of course!

D

DALE, GEORGE. Arrived at Stamford Bridge from Scottish club side Kilmarnock in 1919. Dale was a fine wing-half, who tended to be somewhat adventurous when under pressure. In Scotland his trickery was seen as cheeky confidence, in England it was all too often viewed as arrogance. Dale was a fine footballer who was perhaps a little ahead of his time.

D'ARCY, SEAMUS. Otherwise known as 'Jimmy'. Seamus arrived at Chelsea via Charlton Athletic. A striker, he had been brought to the Valley in March 1948 from Irish club side, Ballymena. Signed for Chelsea in October 1951 and went on to make 23 league appearances and score 12 goals. He was a quick, lively player who had to work hard at his game. A Northern Ireland International he gained 2 further caps for his country whilst with the Blues, making a career total of 5. He was transferred to Brentford in October 1952.

DAVIES, GORDON. 'Ivor' as he was affectionately known, was a hardworking and busy little forward who was signed from Fulham in November 1984. Davies actually scored on his full debut and produced a hat-trick at Everton just 14 days later. Sadly, those 4 goals were followed by just two more in his brief stay at Stamford Bridge. He made 13 first-team appearances before being sold to Manchester City in October 1985.

DEAL—GOOD. Fewer deals have been as astute as that of goalkeeper Alex Stepney. The keeper was with Chelsea for just 112 days in 1966 having been purchased from Millwall for a fee of £50,000. Stepney made one appearance for the Chelsea first eleven before being sold to Manchester United on 13 September 1966 for £55,000. He must have greatly impressed in that one appearance!

DEFEAT. Heaviest defeat on record occurred on 26 September 1953, in a 1st Division fixture at Stamford Bridge against Wolverhampton Wanderers. Chelsea 1 Wolves 8.

On a brighter note, Chelsea have also inflicted Wigan Athletic's heaviest defeat in an FA Cup 3rd round replay at Springfield Park, Wigan on 26 January 1985. Final score; Wigan 0 Chelsea 5.

DEFEATS—FEWEST. Club record in one season stands at 5 defeats in 46 games. Football League division 2, 1988/89 season. Not surprisingly, Chelsea were Champions of the said League that season.

DEMPSEY, JOHN. Born in Hampstead and signed for Fulham in March 1964, big John played some 149 games and scored 4 goals whilst at Craven Cottage, before making the short journey to Stamford Bridge in January 1969. A dependable player who scored relatively few goals, just 7 in 200 Blues games, he remembers with some pleasure one particular strike in the 1971 European Cup Winners Cup replay when Real Madrid were beaten 3–2 on aggregate. It was Johnno's goal which made the difference, a cracking volley giving Borja in Real's goal no chance. Injury-prone, he moved to America in March 1978 to play in their soccer leagues. John Dempsey was Mister Reliable, made few mistakes because he always took the safe option. He made 19 appearances for the Republic of Ireland and also won an FA Cup winner's medal in 1970.

DICKENS, ALAN. Fine ball player and smooth operator in midfield, Dickens arrived at Chelsea after many outstanding performances for London rivals, West Ham United, where he made 192 first-team outings. Signed for Chelsea in August 1989 and hardly made an impact on the side. On a good day he was innovative, and made the ball talk; on a bad day, and there were many at Chelsea, he failed to get involved in the action. After just 46 games and 4 goals he was freed to Brentford in February 1993.

DICKS, ALAN. Dicks was hardly what one could call a player of any great note. Signed for Chelsea in September 1951 having previously turned out for Dulwich Hamlet, Rainham Town, and Millwall as an amateur. His appearances for Chelsea were infrequent as inconsistency was his great flaw. Despite this he was part of the Championship winning side of 1955, making just one appearance that season. A Chelsea career total of 33 league appearances were made with just the one goal between 1951 and November 1958 when he was sold to Southend United. He later played for Coventry City before a career in the coaching and management side of the game with a number of clubs.

DICKSON, WILLIAM. Tall, elegant wing-half from Glenavon, Ireland. Bill Dickson first appeared for Notts County having signed for the Magpies shortly after the end of the Second World War, November 1945 to be precise. A strong and competitive player, he quickly earned a good reputation in England. November 1947 saw him move to London and Chelsea. His consistent play and eagerness to win the ball endeared him to the fans as he continued to improve. He made 101 league appearances and scored 2 goals before being transferred to Arsenal in October 1953, and later played for Mansfield Town.

DIGWEED, PERRY. Goalkeeper signed on loan from Brighton and Hove Albion during the 1987/88 season. He was an uninspiring keeper with an apparent dislike for the crossed ball. Digweed returned to Brighton after just 3 games for the club. Also had loan spells at West Bromwich

Albion, Charlton Athletic, Newcastle United and Wimbledon, mainly as cover.

DIXON, KERRY. Born in Luton, this strong, athletic striker was something of a sensation at his first league club, Reading, for whom he signed in July 1980. At Elm Park he banged in 51 goals in 116 outings which was sufficient for Chelsea to snap him up in August 1983. Kerry was an instant hit at Stamford Bridge, his goals and strength were likened to those of Bobby Tambling and Dixon relished the glory of the limelight even though the majority of his goals were provided for him rather than self-motivated efforts. Despite this, he was a finisher, as clinical as the best of them. He gained International recognition with England, earning 8 full caps between 1985–86, played 413 games for the club and scored 193 goals. He was bitterly disappointed not to break Tambling's overall scoring record of 202 goals. In July 1992 he was sold to Southampton for £575,000 and later moved back to his home town Luton, where he is still banging in the goals.

DOCHERTY, JAMES. Scottish-born striker signed from East Stirling in March 1979. Docherty was to make just 2 appearances for the first team before returning to Scotland with Dundee United. Without being too disrespectful to Docherty, he played his best football in Scotland, and seemed out of his depth at Chelsea.

DOCHERTY, THOMAS. Team manager January 1962 – October 1967. The Doc was and still is a real character in the game. As a player he starred for Celtic, Preston North End and Arsenal before arriving at Stamford Bridge in 1961 when he took on a player/coach role. Docherty took Chelsea down into the 2nd Division in his first season in charge, through no fault of his own I hasten to add, but more the legacy of Ted Drake. The following year the Blues were back where they belonged, in the 1st Division. Docherty worked wonders, but was a strict master, dictating what players could and couldn't do: if anyone dared breach his regulations then it was a fine or similar internal

Kerry Dixon

punishment. Those who questioned his decisions, especially if they were not qualified to do so, were given short shrift and advised to keep their opinions to themselves. Chelsea had but one manager during 'The Doc's' reign. Rightly or wrongly his discipline code was strict and he would never have allowed his players to conduct themselves in the manner some present-day players do.

Under his command the club won the Football League Cup in 1965 and were runners-up in the 1967 FA Cup. He resigned as manager after internal politics forced his hand.

He later managed Rotherham United, Queen's Park Rangers, Aston Villa, FC Oporto, Scotland, Manchester United, Derby County, Queen's Park Rangers (again), Preston North End, Wolverhampton Wanderers and Altrincham. There was also a spell in Australia. Docherty was very much his own man with a knowledge of the game second to none. Today he is an after-dinner speaker and very much a gentleman when one meets him.

DOLDING, LEN. Born in Belgium, this speedy and tricky little winger first signed for Wealdstone before Chelsea plucked him from the relative obscurity of the non-league game shortly after the end of the Second World War. Dolding was also a first-class cricketer with Middlesex, proving his all-round ability as a sportsman. As one would expect from such a fit player, Dolding was a terrific sprinter, although his sprints down the Chelsea wing were few and far between. He made just 26 league appearances and scored 2 goals. He was sold to Norwich City in July 1948.

DONAGHY, MAL. Northern Ireland International defender whose playing career started at Luton Town. Donaghy is a defender of real quality, and has been a marvellous servant to each of his other clubs, namely, Manchester United and Luton Town.

His knowledge and all-round enthusiasm virtually ensure that once his playing days are over he could make the move into club management. In the twilight of his career, Donaghy's clear love for the game is visible in each and every performance.

DORIGO, ANTHONY. A tremendous left-back, Dorigo was a footballer of real quality. Quick, skilful and reliable, he signed for the Blues from Aston Villa in 1987 in a £475,000 deal. Few players of the modern era have such a delightful touch or equally, such a power-packed accurate shot.

It is incredible that Dorigo has not made more full International appearances for his country, everyone, except the England manager, seems to applaud Dorigo's play. A move to Leeds came about in 1991 for a £1.3 million fee,

Tony Dorigo

which was more of a loss to Chelsea than initially appeared; Dorigo has never been successfully replaced to this day.

DOW, ANDREW. Midfield player, born in Dundee in 1973. Dow is an exceptional talent whose playing career began in the Scottish junior leagues where he had made a name for himself playing with Sporting Club 85. Dundee signed him in 1990 and he made his league debut during the 1991/92 season. As time progressed he seemed to mature, so much so that Chelsea signed him in August 1993. Since then he

THE STAMFORD BRIDGE ENCYCLOPEDIA

has broken into the first team on several occasions and looks to have a bright future ahead of him.

DOWNING, SAMUEL. In the early days of football, certainly during the Edwardian era, footballers were judged by different standards from today's. Sam Downing, a wing-half and a real terrier was described by one journal of the day as: 'a gentleman who passes the ball freely, when chasing the ball his play is fair and clean'. Downing actually signed for Chelsea at the beginning of the 1910/11 season and as a trialist proved himself a useful defender.

DRAKE, EDWARD. Team manager May 1952 – September 1961. As a player Ted Drake was fast, furious, and brave. An England International, his career began in earnest with Winchester City, before a dream move to his home town club, Southampton in November 1931. His goalscoring skills were noticed by Arsenal who signed him up in March 1934. Drake was a prolific goalscorer, one of Britain's best, who, in a single game for Arsenal on 14 December 1935, scored 7 goals against Aston Villa at Villa Park. Few professionals to this day can claim to have scored so many goals in one first-class competitive fixture. Drake came to Chelsea as manager and took over an ailing side, transforming them into league champions in no time at all. The manager brought in fresh, young blood, such as one James Greaves; equally as prolific in front of goal as the great man himself. It was perhaps Drake's greatest downfall that he placed too much emphasis on bringing youths through into the first team. The inexperience of his playing staff eventually cost him his job, with the club results in the 1961/62 season hardly promising.

After leaving Stamford Bridge he worked as a bookmaker before he moved to Spain as assistant manager of Barcelona in January 1970, but returned to England in June the same year. He also played cricket for Hampshire between 1931–1936 proving his great sporting all-round ability. Honours include, 8 FA Cup winners medals, and one Football League Champions medal, plus 5 full International caps for England.

DRAWS. Highest-scoring draws in football league fixtures to date are:
1937 v Bolton Wanderers 5–5
1966 v West Ham United 5–5.

DRAWS. Highest-scoring draws in first-class domestic competition are:
1958 v Darlington 3–3
1985 v Sheffield Wednesday 4–4.

DRIVER, PHILLIP. Gangly, slim-line striker, signed by Geoff Hurst from Wimbledon in September 1980. A lad whose heart was in the game but whose mind often wasn't. Driver was hardly a sensational forward and was not in the Geoff Hurst mould. Yet there was something about the player which endeared him to many Chelsea fans, he scored the odd goal, and seemed determined enough, but could never be described as a classic footballer. He played 25 games for the club before returning to Wimbledon in July 1983. He later drifted out of the professional game and into the non-league game.

DROY, MICHAEL. A career that began with Slough Town before a move to the Bridge in September 1970. Micky Droy was a huge defender, 6′ 4″ tall and weighing in at around 15 stone. He was a strong tackler, dominant in the air, and had a heart as big as an ox. Droy's desire to win and his commitment saw the Blues through many a rough patch. He inspired those around him, and frightened the opposition to death with his blank stare. His leadership qualities brought him the team captaincy until March 1985, when he was transferred to Crystal Palace in a move which greatly disappointed many Chelsea fans. Droy was a giant, on and off the field, a real character and an ambassador for the game with his caring attitude towards fans outside Stamford Bridge. Many a time have I seen him surrounded by autograph hunters and Micky would not disappoint one of them, remaining there until he had signed every one. Few footballers would show such honesty and dedication.

DUBERRY, MICHAEL. Another promising youngster, Michael Duberry signed for the club in June 1993. A defender, he made his full debut against Coventry City in May 1994. He is currently learning his trade in the reserves but will no doubt soon fit in with first-team plans.

DUBLIN, KEITH. Quick and highly-rated full-back, who made his full league debut for Chelsea towards the end of the 1983/84 season. He was somewhat unfortunate to find himself out of the first team. When he eventually broke through and maintained some kind of decent form it seemed that his name would be next to the number 3 on the first-team sheet each week. All things must come to an end and when Tony Dorigo and Clive Wilson were signed Dublin was allowed to leave, joining Brighton and Hove Albion in 1987.

DURIE, GORDON. Scottish International and renowned striker, Gordon Durie was a resilient, and above all, tough forward. His pace and dogged determination often created half-chances in front of goal. He was signed from Hibernian in a £380,000 deal in 1986 and proved to be as prolific as Tambling, as skilful as Cooke, as hard as 'Chopper' Harris, and as inconsistent as refereeing decisions. Durie could be wonderful, he could also be lethargic and seemingly uninterested. With the ball at his feet and his head down, off he would go, the only thought in his mind being to score a goal. All too often he squandered chances when a simple pass to a better-placed colleague could have earned a simple goal. Having said that, the goals he did score were often spectacular to say the least. Durie remained at Chelsea until 1991, when he was sold to rivals, Tottenham Hotspur. A terrace idol had been and gone, Durie's style and swagger will long be remembered within the seats of Stamford Bridge, the mention of his name will bring a smile to many Chelsea fans. Durie was that kind of footballer; everybody criticised him, but everyone loved him. He is currently playing for Glasgow Rangers, and still scoring sensational goals!

Gordon Durie

E

ELLIOTT, PAUL. Arrived from Glasgow Celtic in July 1991 for a fee of £1.4 million pounds. Elliott was a vastly experienced central defender, tall and domineering in the heart of the Chelsea rearguard, hardly anything got past him in the air. In a career that began in South London with Charlton Athletic, Paul moved to Luton Town in 1983 before a relatively short journey up the M1 to Aston Villa in March 1985. The Villa Park experience was followed by a European adventure at Pisa where his play shone in the difficult Italian leagues. A return to British shores came about in the 1989/90 season when Celtic literally pipped several top clubs to his signature before Chelsea finally got their man two years later. Elliott was subjected to a crunching career-wrecking tackle during the early part of the 1992/93 season, a cruel end to a good career. Elliott made a total of 54 appearances for the Blues and scored just 3 goals.

ELMES, TIMOTHY. Born in Croydon in 1962, Tim Elmes had high hopes and great ambition. As a midfielder he could at times dictate the type and style of game in the junior and youth teams. He signed professional forms for the club in July 1980 and was drafted into the first eleven almost immediately when injuries and suspensions dictated so. Elmes struggled to make any serious impact in his 2 first-team appearances; his enthusiasm was obvious, but this is not always sufficient to see one through. Elmes was released to Leyton Orient later that season but never made a full first-team appearance.

ESCAPE—LUCKY. Without doubt the luckiest escape the club have ever had occurred in the 1950/51 season. At that time the club were struggling to find form and matters deteriorated with a run of just 5 points gained from a possible 28. By April 1951 the writing was on the wall, Chelsea were almost certain to be relegated. However, in an amazing turn around the team actually won their last four league fixtures; 1–0 at home to Liverpool, 2–1 at home to Wolves, 2–1 at Fulham and 4–0 at home to Bolton. They ended the season third bottom of the 1st Division with the same number of points (32) as Sheffield Wednesday and Everton below them. Through the goal average ruling, Chelsea escaped relegation by 0.044 of a goal!

EUROPEAN CUP. When Chelsea won the 1st Division Championship in 1955 the club declined to take part in the European Cup. They were replaced by Gwardia Warsaw. It was the competition's inaugural season, and there was some apprehension as to its feasibility, thus the Chelsea refusal. Incidentally, for the record, Gwardia Warsaw went out in the first round, losing 4–1 on aggregate to Djurgarden!

EUROPEAN VICTORY. The biggest ever European victory to be recorded stands at a ridiculous 21–0 aggregate victory by Chelsea over Jeunesse Hautcharage of Luxembourg in the European Cup Winners Cup of 1971. It is unlikely that such a scoreline will occur ever again.

EVANS, ROBERT. Strong wing-half signed from Celtic in May 1960, Bobby had made an outstanding name for himself in the Scottish game. As an International, he earned some 48 caps for his country. When he arrived at Stamford Bridge he was, in fact, 33 years of age and his signing was very much a gamble by the Chelsea management. Evans though, was a quality player and although there were occasions when his pace was questionable, his commitment and experience were outstanding. Despite this he remained at the Bridge for the one season (1960/61) and made 32 appearances. He moved on to Newport County in June 1961 where he was player/manager.

EXHAUSTION. Saturday, 29 October 1932, will long remain a unique date in Chelsea's proud history. On this date the team faced Blackpool in a 1st Division fixture at Bloomfield Road, Blackpool. The weather conditions for the game were appalling, blizzardous wind with driving rain, yet the pitch, according to the match officials was playable. The wind played havoc with the football which swirled and ballooned with every cross or powerful kick. Chelsea, playing against the blizzard in the second half, literally collapsed. No less than five players were forced to leave the field suffering from exhaustion through fighting against the gale blowing towards them. With just six Blues players remaining at the end of 90 minutes, it is little surprise that they lost the game 1–0.

F

FALCO, MARK. Arrived on loan from Tottenham Hotspur in November 1982. Falco had been a bright talent at White Hart Lane, another who had somehow lost his way. Falco linked up with Hoddle on many occasions and on a good day the pair were electric. Falco, though, was not as skilful nor as committed as Hoddle, thus, when he lost his first-team place in 1982, the responsibility lay with him to win it back. The loan spell at Chelsea was a short one, just 3 games before being recalled by Spurs where he regained his first-team spot and played with a great deal more consistency. He later played for Watford, Queen's Park Rangers, Rangers and Millwall.

FANZINES. Several totally independent titles exist and are sold outside the ground on matchdays. The choice of Chelsea fanzines is excellent depending upon supporters' own opinions and impressions. The main fanzines to be found on the Fulham Road are *The Chelsea Independent*, *Cockney Rebel*, *The Red Card* and *Weststanders*. All provide an alternative and unofficial view of matters relating to the club. I make no preference as to quality or value for money, leaving that to the fanzine support and experts.

FASCIONE, JOSEPH. Signed from Kirkintilloch Rob Roy in October 1962, Fascione was a flying winger who remained at the Bridge for three years but failed to suitably impress. He made a total of just 27 appearances, and scored one goal.

FEELY, PETER. Ex-Enfield striker who was signed in May 1970. Feely had been an England Youth and England amateur representative whilst in the non-league game and so possessed suitable qualifications to turn professional. A rather clumsy striker he made just 4 first-team outings scoring 2 goals before being sold to Bournemouth in February 1973.

FERRIS, JAMES. International with Northern Ireland, Jimmy Ferris was signed by the club from Belfast City in the 1920/21 season. Ferris was an instant hit and scored some 15 goals for the club during that first season. In 1921 he added to his International honours by representing Northern Ireland against England and Wales. Ferris was a rough-and-ready striker who always made time to speak to his fans. He eventually returned home to Belfast where he rejoined City and continued to score goals for them.

FILLERY, MICHAEL. An outstanding performer in the Chelsea midfield of the late 1970s. Fillery progressed through the Youth team and was a marvellous asset to the club. He signed professional in August 1978. Strong and calm, he was something of a robust footballer getting in where it hurt and refusing to concede defeat. His gutsy performances for the club made him something of a terrace hero. He made a total of 176 appearances for the club and scored 41 goals before a move to Queen's Park Rangers in August 1983.

FINALS AT STAMFORD BRIDGE. Stamford Bridge has been used for three FA Cup Finals:
1920 Aston Villa v Huddersfield Town 1–0
Attendance: 50,018
1921 Tottenham Hotspur v Wolverhampton Wanderers 1–0
Attendance: 72,805

1922 Huddersfield Town v Preston North End 1–0
Attendance: 53,000

FINES. Although most clubs receive various fines from the various leagues in which they play, two of Chelsea's worst have been in recent years. In 1988 when, according to the Football League, they failed to prevent crowd trouble in a fixture against Middlesbrough on 28 May 1988, a fine of £75,000 was charged against the club. Further to this, in January 1991 when the Football League again fined the club, this time for alleged irregular payments to players, the fine was an astronomical £105,000. Tough penalties when compared with others handed out to individuals in recent times!

FINNIESTON, STEPHEN. Scottish-born forward signed in December 1971 through the apprentice set-up. Finnieston was an old fashioned-style striker, strong and prepared to run and run until he dropped. Although he lacked finesse his method and running off the ball created opportunities for himself and his colleagues. After a Chelsea career total of 86 appearances and 37 goals he was sold to Sheffield United in June 1978 when other more classy strikers arrived on the scene.

FLECK, ROBERT. Diminutive striker who struggled to make any impact at the club. At Norwich, his previous club, he had been influential in their strike force which had persuaded Chelsea to pay £2.1 million pounds for his talents in 1992. The move seemed to affect him greatly, gone was the desperado and cavalier style of play which had earned him such a good reputation and 4 full International caps for Scotland. Fleck never lived up to expectations and struggled during his time at the club. The reasons behind this will never be known, a player of his quality should not suddenly stop displaying class, yet Fleck did. To his credit he maintained enthusiasm and a desire to regain form but it never arrived.

FLYING—HIGH. On 19 April 1957 (Good Friday) Chelsea became the first ever team to fly home from one domestic

Robert Fleck

league fixture in order to play another. Having played Newcastle United at St James' Park the team caught a plane home to face Everton at the Bridge the following day. The team won both games, 2–1 at Newcastle and 5–1 against Everton.

FOULKE, WILLIAM. Probably the best known Chelsea player of all time, and no wonder. Standing at 6′ 6″ tall and weighing 22 stones, Foulke was hardly what one could describe as athletic. Despite his giant size, Foulke was agile and probably one of the best keepers Chelsea have ever had. He would yell instructions to his defenders and, often, attackers, from his goal, and was a worthy captain of the side. Indeed, Foulke was Chelsea's first ever captain. An England International he gained one cap in 1897 against Wales. One journalist of the era claimed that he could punch the ball farther than many players could kick it. More humorous, was this striker's riposte to a colleague who had begged him to cross the ball to him from an ideal wing position, 'I could see nothing but an eclipse of the sun as he ran out of his goal toward me, there wasn't enough room between both ends of the ground to get the ball across to you!' Humour apart, Foulke's career had taken him to Alfreton, Blackwell Colliery (his home town), Sheffield United, Chelsea in May 1905, before a move to Bradford City in April 1906 from where he retired from the game the following year. He also played cricket on four occasions for Derbyshire in 1900. His honours included, Football League Champions 1898, FA Cup Winner, 1899, 1902, and losing finalist in 1901. He died in May 1916 suffering from pneumonia. A real character and a man who could hold his head high in the knowledge that he was an ambassador for the game.

FRANCIS, STEPHEN. Goalkeeping can be a difficult art to master, some make saves look easy, others struggle to attain such a cool, calm and collected image. Steve Francis, although a great shot-stopper was not particularly outstanding in the fields of calmness and leadership in his penalty area. He was signed from the youth side as a professional in April 1982. As a youngster he represented England Youth which is an early indication of his ability. Francis did put in some fine performances during his 4-plus years as a professional at the club, but he lacked that little something extra which would have made him one of the country's top keepers. He was sold to Reading in February 1987 and forged a fine career for himself at Elm Park.

FREEMAN, CHARLES. Battling forward who played some fine football in the early part of the second decade of the

20th Century. Freeman was slight and fleet of foot, his link play with Vivian Woodward and George Hilsdon was in itself a sight to behold. Freeman could often pop up with the odd vital goal himself including his solo strike against Bradford in April 1912 which won the game and put Chelsea back in the 1st Division.

FREESTONE, ROGER. Goalkeeper who made his way along the M4 in April 1987 when he signed from Newport County. Some called him 'Man Mountain' as his huge frame filled a great gap between the Chelsea sticks. Freestone was assertive and dominant in his area, except when a crossed ball came in, then he would take a back seat and rely on his defence to head clear. This was his one weakness as a keeper, a man of his height should have had no problem with the gathering of the crossed ball, but his lack of experience meant that he was often punished for such failures. His lack of good fortune and a poor run of results saw him ousted from first-team keeper position and eventually moved to his native Wales to play for Swansea City in September 1991. Today he is a much more accomplished keeper, learning his trade in the lower leagues has proved very fruitful.

FREW, JAMES. Tall and confident defender whose contribution in the heart of the Chelsea defence was outstanding. Frew had proved himself an able defender in the early 1920s when drafted into an injury-hit squad, he played well alongside Harry Wilding. Both players organised the defence so well that the club could boast of the tightest back four in the football league.

FRIDGE, LESLIE. Scottish-born keeper who signed through the apprentice ranks in September 1985. Fridge made just one appearance for the Blues in that same season. Hardly a distinguished Chelsea career, he was, all the same, a reasonable keeper having appeared for Scotland as a Youth and U21 substitute.

FROST, LEE. Winger who hailed from Woking and signed through the youth team in July 1976. He made his league debut against Aston Villa in April 1978 and went on to make 12 full appearances for the club scoring 5 goals in the process. He eventually moved to Brentford in December 1980.

FURLONG, PAUL. Tall, stocky striker, Paul Furlong made a name for himself on the non-league circuit with Enfield. One goal against Kettering Town saw him dribble his way past six players before slotting the ball past a helpless Kettering keeper. This goal killed off Town's title hopes, but was a tremendous piece of skill.

A move to Coventry City followed in July 1991 then a move to Vicarage Road, Watford, twelve months later. Some 40 goals later he was signed in a £2.3 million deal by Chelsea in June 1994. At the moment this seems to be hanging like a millstone around his neck. Furlong has thus far rarely shown true value for money, although there is a feeling that given a couple of seasons to mature and settle in he will prove to be a prolific goalscorer. Only time will tell.

Paul Furlong

G

GALLACHER, HUGH. The great Hughie Gallacher was signed by Chelsea in one of the shock transfers of the 1930s. Gallacher was hero worshipped on Tyneside by the fanatical Geordie support of Newcastle United. Whilst with the Magpies he made a total of 174 appearances and scored an incredible 143 goals. He was red hot, and the most revered striker of his time. Chelsea paid £10,000 for his services in the summer of 1930. His first game for the Blues was a league fixture at St James' Park when 68,586 people turned out to pay homage to their idol. Chelsea lost the game 1–0. It was claimed that a further 40,000 were locked out, unable to get in to see the game! A tiny striker, he was incredibly powerful and, of course, a great asset to such a player, he was awkward to handle. Too much pressure and he would go down in the penalty box, too little and he would turn you inside out. His weakness was his fiery temper. On more than one occasion he swore at and verbally abused match officials to such an extent that some defenders would try to wind him up. His football career began with Queen of the South before a move to Airdrie, then Newcastle United. At Chelsea he made some 132 league appearances and scored 72 goals. He later moved to Derby County, Notts County and Grimsby Town, before returning to Tyneside with Gateshead.

In June 1957 Hughie Gallacher committed suicide by jumping in front of the York-Edinburgh express train at the appropriately named, 'Dead Man's Crossing', Low Fell. With his life in tatters and an embarrassing court case impending he could take no more. It was a sad end to a career which had thrilled and brought so much enjoyment and satisfaction to so many.

GARLAND, CHRISTOPHER. Blond-haired striker of the Seventies, Chris Garland was signed in September 1971 from Bristol City where he grabbed 31 league goals in 142 appearances.

At Chelsea, Garland became something of a hero before he even kicked a football. He was quick and evasive on the ball and had good passing ability. He made some 111 appearances and scored 31 goals before an expensive transfer to Leicester City in February 1975. He later returned to Bristol City.

GARNER, WILLIAM. At Notts County, Bill Garner must have thought that he had failed to meet the required standards to become a successful professional footballer. He was released by County and played for Bedford Town for almost three years before Southend United signed him in November 1969. Having scored with some frequency at Roots Hall, Garner was signed by Chelsea in September 1972. Some believed him to be cumbersome in front of goal, but Garner was a deceptive player; nimble and strong he could hold off the most violent of challenges and lay off the ball to a colleague. In the air he could be lethal, with a bullet-like header; he was as dangerous a forward as Chelsea have ever had. He scored 36 goals in 105 appearances and moved to Cambridge United in November 1978.

GIBBS, DEREK. Signed through the juniors, Derek Gibbs was an inside-forward who tended to lose his impetus when knocked off the ball. Hardly a fighter or a ball winner, he was a finely-tuned footballer who could perform with some exquisite skill when everything went right. However, more often than not he found it difficult to reproduce consistent form. Turned professional in April 1955 and made 25 appearances and scored 6 goals before moving to Leyton Orient in November 1960.

GILLIES, MATT. Elegant centre-half who made 145 league appearances for Bolton Wanderers between 1946–1951. His career had been badly interrupted by the war and it was during this period that he made a guest appearance for Chelsea in the war-time leagues. After the war he returned to Burnden Park and later played for Leicester City.

GOALS. Jimmy Greaves was just 20 years and 261 days old when he scored his 100th league goal for Chelsea in a fixture against Manchester City on 19 November 1960.

GOALS—BURST OF. In a 1st Division fixture at Stamford Bridge on 14 October 1978 against Bolton Wanderers, the Blues were losing 3–0 with just 15 minutes remaining. In an incredible burst of goals Chelsea scored 4 times to win the game 4–3.

GOAL—FIRST EVER. Chelsea's first ever league goal was scored by player/manager, John Robertson in a 1–0 win at Blackpool on 9 September 1905.

GOALS—IN ONE SEASON. The most goals Chelsea have ever scored in one season stands at 98 in the 1st division 1960/61 season.

GOALS—5 SCORED IN A SINGLE GAME. Three players have managed incredible scoring feats for the club, bagging 5 goals in single games.

George Hilsdon v Glossop 1 September 1906
Jimmy Greaves v Wolves 30 August 1958
Jimmy Greaves v Preston 19 December 1959
Jimmy Greaves v West Brom 3 December 1960
Bobby Tambling v Aston Villa 17 September 1966

GODDEN, ANTHONY. Goalkeeper who sprung to fame playing for West Bromwich Albion where he turned in some exemplary performances. Godden was not the tallest of goalkeepers but he was strong, agile, and brave. Like all players, he could be rather temperamental and made the odd bloomer. Such errors eventually cost him his first place at Albion and, after two loan spells at Luton Town and Walsall respectively, he signed for Chelsea in March 1986. A good, reflex keeper he seemed a worthy acquisition and the fans took to his often extrovert style. Sadly his days at the Bridge were numbered as Birmingham City came for him in July 1987 and, to everyone's surprise, Godden left having made just 38 appearances.

GOULDEN, LEONARD. Inside-forward who was neat and attractive on the ball. He was later given a coaching role at Stamford Bridge in 1950–1952. Goulden was an England International with 14 caps and also represented his country at schoolboy level. Signed from West Ham United in August 1945, he made 99 league appearances and scored 17 goals in his Blues career. Some writers of the day claimed he was the best inside-forward of his time. After his Chelsea career finished he moved to Watford as manager/coach. He later had a spell coaching abroad in Libya before returning to England first with Banbury, and then as trainer/coach with Oxford United.

GRAHAM, GEORGE. A midfielder-cum-striker who was signed from Aston Villa in July 1964. Georgie was a keen and exquisite player, his first touch and body swerve in those early days left many defenders in his wake. A smashing character, he projected a rather dour image during games, but this was largely due to his commitment and concentration. He scored some 46 goals in 102 appearances for Chelsea and was a great favourite with the fans until he signed for Arsenal in September 1966, the rest as they say, is history. Graham had a splendid career at Highbury and later moved to Manchester United, Portsmouth, and Crystal Palace. As a manager he built a rock-solid Millwall side before moving back to Highbury as team manager.

Despite the accusations recently levelled at him about 'bungs', etc. George Graham is still one of the nicest characters and big stars of the modern game. Few top managers go out of their way to speak to supporters, George did, and he enjoyed it too. He was also a Scottish International player with 12 full caps, U23 honours and Schoolboy International honours.

GRAY, WILLIAM. An out and out winger with an asute left foot. Bill Gray started out as an amateur with Wolverhampton Wanderers, then moved to Gateshead. He signed for Leyton Orient in May 1947 after a spell with Dinnington Colliery. He signed for Chelsea in March 1949 and went on to make 146 league appearances, scoring 12 goals. He made two FA Cup semi-final appearances for Chelsea, on the losing side on both occasions before being sold to Burnley for £16,000 in August 1953. Later he played for Nottingham Forest and became player-manager of Millwall. He also managed Brentford and Notts County before a move to Fulham as coach.

GREAVES, JAMES. Jimmy Greaves was all things to all men. Idol, heart-throb and fantastic footballer. Now a high-profile media character known for speaking his mind, Jimmy Greaves was a Chelsea junior before signing professional in May 1957. His 169 appearances and an incredible 132 goals speak volumes for his abilities. An inside-forward, he was not the fastest of players, however his incredible ball control and strength at fielding challenges provided him with no end of goal-scoring opportunities. Greavsie could hit them with either foot, left, right, high or low, he was devastating in front of goal. The incredible thing about Jimmy Greaves was his apparent lack of enthusiasm and commitment for the full 90 minutes. No matter what has been said about him in the past, he was, in most games, somewhat innocuous for about 80–85 minutes, but in the remaining 5 minutes he could be lethal. He could destroy teams with his deadly accurate shooting. He was sold to AC Milan in June 1961, a move he openly regrets to this day and just six months later he was back in England with Tottenham Hotspur where his goal-scoring prowess continued to impress: 220 league goals in 321 appearances. He later played for West Ham United. An England International, he gained 57 full caps for his country and represented England at Youth and U23 levels.

GREENWOOD, RONALD. A reasonably nondescript player, yet a super team manager, Ron Greenwood's football career began at Chelsea in October 1943. A powerful and not so elegant centre-half, he never broke into the first team and moved on to Bradford Park Avenue in December 1945. After a couple of seasons at Bradford, where he dominated in defence, Greenwood returned to London having been bought by Brentford in March 1949. His only league goal in 142 league appearances was scored for Brentford. His aerial dominance again attracted Chelsea who bought him back in October 1952. However, he was, in effect, just another centre-half, there were no outstanding features to his game other than his ability to defend and marshall those around him. He was transferred to Fulham in February 1955.

As a manager he worked at Eastbourne United, then became assistant manager at Arsenal, England Youth and U23 manager, West Ham United manager and then England team manager. Greenwood's best days were undoubtedly his time in charge at West Ham when the Hammers won the FA Cup in 1964, the European Cup Winners Cup in 1965, and were runners-up in the Football League Cup in 1966. As a player he won a Championship medal with Chelsea in 1955, and one England 'B' International cap.

GULLIT, RUUD. Without being too dismissive of other Chelsea players, the signing of Ruud Gullit has to be one of the biggest and best things to occur at Stamford Bridge for many a season. A midfield genius, Gullit is good with the ball at his feet or flying at it with his head. Gullit originally played for Meerboys and DWS as a youth team player before making a move into the big time with Haarlem. There then followed spells with Feyenoord, PSV Eindhoven, before a move to AC Milan for a then world record fee of £6 million in 1987.

H

HALES, KEVIN. Midfielder from Dartford, Hales was yet another product of the excellent youth team set up, signing professional terms in January 1979. Hales was a victim of his own success, a raw talent who was not quite good enough for a permanent first-team place yet who attracted the attention of some lesser sides. He made just 25 first-team appearances before moving to Leyton Orient in August 1983.

HALL, GARETH. Solid and tough-tackling defender, Hall is a full Welsh International and a fine distributor of the ball. His no-nonsense style has ruffled many quality forwards who find him difficult to beat. There can be no doubt as to his credentials for the future. One of a handful of defenders who one could say are among the elite in the Premier League.

HALSE, HAROLD. England International inside-forward, Halse was hardly a big man, but his size mattered little when he was given half an opportunity in front of goal. Born in Leytonstone, he first played for Newportians (Leyton), Wanstead, Barking Town, Clapton Orient, Southend United, then Manchester United in 1907. He was impressive at Old Trafford and remained there until a move to Aston Villa in July 1912 where he was part of the successful 1913 FA Cup winning side. In May of that same year he signed for Chelsea and again appeared in an FA Cup final, this time as losing finalist in the Khaki Final of 1915. He moved to Charlton Athletic in 1921.

HAMILTON, IAN. Chico Hamilton went on to make his claim for fame and glory elsewhere. As a young apprentice at the Blues, he was keen and full of exuberance, but he managed just 3 first-team appearances and scored only 2 goals. He moved to Southend United in September 1968, where he gained further experience, enough to satisfy Aston Villa that he was just what they needed. At Villa his status become almost legendary. Today supporters still discuss 'Chico's' skill on the ball and dexterity when sprinting forward.

HARFORD, MICHAEL. Hard, robust forward, signed from Luton Town in August 1992 for a fee of around £300,000. Mick Harford was a vastly experienced player, a predator in front of goal and one of the era's most consistent goalscorers. Everywhere he has played he has scored goals; Lincoln City, Newcastle United, Bristol City, Birmingham City, Luton Town (twice), Derby County. At Chelsea things were no different, albeit he was allegedly in the twilight of his career. His stay at the Bridge was but a brief one, 7 months to be precise, in that time he proved a big hit with the fans and bagged 11 goals in 33 appearances. In March 1993 he was sold to Sunderland for a £250,000 fee. Twelve months later came a move to Coventry City before a return to the nation's capital at Wimbledon where he is still a regular in the first team and is one of the Dons' leading goalscorers! He has two full International caps with England.

HARMER, THOMAS. A wizard on the ball, it was Chelsea's great misfortune that they never saw the best of this effervescent character. Harmer, an East Ender, first signed for Tottenham Hotspur in August 1948. It was at White

Hart Lane that he played his best football. A neat passer and all-rounder, he had what it takes to motivate those around him. He made over 200 appearances for Spurs before moving to Watford in October 1960. Tommy finally came to Chelsea aged 34 in September 1962 and made just enough appearances for the Blues for those who witnessed him to appreciate his talent and undoubted skills.

HARRIS, ALAN. Left-back Alan Harris is one of the few players to have been at the club on two separate occasions, which tends to speak for itself. A hard character who made 98 appearances for the club between June 1960–November 1964, when he was sold to Coventry City, and May 1966–July 1967. As a schoolboy he gained recognition at Youth and England International level. Later he played for Queen's Park Rangers, Plymouth Argyle, and Cambridge United.

HARRIS, JOHN. In a playing career which spanned some 22 years, Johnny Harris excelled himself at five separate clubs. A defender, he was born in Glasgow and first played for Swindon Town as an amateur. Prior to the war he was signed by Tottenham Hotspur then Wolverhampton Wanderers, but never officially kicked a ball in a football league fixture for either of them. Once the war was over and football began to regain some form of normality, he signed for Chelsea in August 1945 and went on to make 326 league appearances, scoring 14 league goals for the Blues. He first played as centre-half at Chelsea, but Ted Drake moved him to full-back, mainly because of his lack of height as a central defender. He was made team captain and was an influential member of the 1955 League Championship winning side.

He moved to Chester City as player/manager in July 1956 and later managed Sheffield United for a period of 14 years, although one of these was as a general manager.

HARRIS, RONALD. 'Chopper' Harris was a real character in the Chelsea camp; hard, dependable, and undeniably loyal, he loved the club and everything about it. Ron was a player who brought a smile to your face, his commitment and dedication made up for any defensive deficiencies he may have had. He signed in November 1961 and led Chelsea to some marvellous victories and honours during his 18 plus years at the club as a player. An outstanding leader of men his guidance and motivation ensured that he would be one of the greatest club captains in Blues history. A magnificent 783 appearances and 14 goals tells you everything you need to know about his game. Very much a defender he once claimed he got a nose bleed if he went into the opposition's penalty area. He was an awesome sight if you were a striker playing against him, with his thick-set frame, but his quick reactions made him equal to the swiftest of players. If there was no chance of dispossessing the striker, then 'Chopper' ensured that the striker had no chance of scoring, all in good spirit of course! After ending his playing days at Brentford, where he acted as player/coach after a transfer in May 1980, he tried his hand at management with Aldershot. Sadly his motivation could not inspire a struggling league team with no money and very little future in the football league at that time. There are many who believe he should have been made manager of Chelsea, especially when others failed to match his credentials for the job!

HARRISON, MICHAEL. Mickey Harrison was a left-winger who relied upon his artistry and trickery to beat his foe. He signed professional for the Blues in April 1957 and was regarded as a real prospect as he could skip past challenges when he flew down the wing. An England Youth and U23 International, he made some 64 appearances between 1957–1962, and scored 9 goals. He was sold to Blackburn Rovers in September 1962 and made 160 league appearances for Rovers, scoring 40 goals. He later played for Plymouth Argyle and Luton Town.

HARROW, JACK. Born in Beddington, Surrey in 1888, Jack Harrow first played his football for Mill Green Rovers then Croydon Common before the move he had dreamed of came up. He signed for Chelsea in April 1911 and was seen as a direct goalscorer, something he had become a dab hand at in Croydon.

However, during training sessions and practise matches, it became clear to the club trainers that Harrow was equally as useful as a centre-half so he was transformed to this role. Still not satisfied that they were getting the best out of him he was tried in several defensive roles before finally settling in at left-back. He gained 2 International caps for England in 1923 and appeared in the 1915 FA Cup final which Chelsea unfortunately lost. As a player he retired in 1926 but joined the backroom training staff at the club, where he remained until 1938. He passed away in July 1958 having worked for Mitcham Council until 1956. Harrow was a deliberate and level-headed player, his favourite move was to delay a final touch until the opposing player committed himself, he would then tap it past him and move forward. A dangerous tactic, but one which he used most successfully.

HAT-TRICK. The record for the most hat-tricks in one season in the football league stands at 6, this was achieved by Jimmy Greaves during the 1960/61 season with Chelsea FC. Incredibly, the previous season he grabbed 3 separate hat-tricks! What price would a player of his ability fetch in today's market?

HATELEY, ANTHONY. One of the most devastating centre-forwards of his time, Hateley, a tall, gangly-looking player, was supreme in the air and powerful on the run. He made goal-scoring look so easy and motivated many youngsters to copy his game.

The striker was 25 years of age when he arrived at Stamford Bridge from Aston Villa in October 1966. At Villa he had grabbed 68 league goals in 127 appearances and was regarded as hot property. For whatever reason, he never truly settled at Chelsea and remained at the club for 9 months, 6 of which were during the football season. His Chelsea record stands at 32 appearances and 9 goals before he moved to Anfield, home of Liverpool FC in July 1967. He also played for Coventry City, Birmingham City, Notts County (twice) and Oldham Athletic.

HAY, DAVID. A real sensation when he signed from Glasgow Celtic in August 1974, David Hay was an uncompromising defender whose qualities lay in his tenacity in the tackle and ferocious leadership and guidance, nothing short of what one would expect from a Scottish full International footballer. Hay made 118 appearances for Chelsea between 1974–1978, and scored 3 goals into the bargain.

HAZARD, MICHAEL. A clever passer of the ball and neat goalscorer, Mickey Hazard had real potential and was a player very much in the mould of Glen Hoddle. With tremendous close control and superb vision he could spread passes all over the pitch with great accuracy and with either foot.

His career began at Tottenham Hotspur before he moved to Chelsea in September 1985. Hazard scored 12 goals for Chelsea, the majority of which were tremendous strikes, either on the volley, or from outside the penalty area. He made 94 first-team outings before being sold to Portsmouth in January 1990.

HEWITT, JOHN. Midfielder signed from Wrexham in the 1912/13 season. Hewitt was a Welsh International who already had 3 full caps behind him when he arrived at Stamford Bridge. His stay in London was but a brief one; enough time for him to make 3 more International appearances in 1913 against England, Scotland and Nigeria before a move North to South Liverpool FC the following year.

HILSDON, GEORGE. Whilst at Chelsea, George Hilsdon gained some 8 England full International caps. He was known locally as George 'Gatling Gun' Hilsdon, mainly because he rattled in goals with incredible frequency.

His career began at East Ham Schools then took him to South West Ham, Clapton Orient, Luton Town in 1902, West Ham United in 1903 and to Chelsea in May 1906. George was the player who virtually the whole nation revered on the football front, his running off the ball and advanced skills would not be out of place in today's game.

Mickey Hazard

His International appearances came against Italy in 1907; Italy, Wales, Scotland, Austria, Bohemia in 1908; and Italy in 1908. He moved to West Ham United in 1912 when it seemed that Chelsea had utilised every ounce of his skill to great advantage. Later he appeared for Chatham in 1919. Many Chelsea fans will be unaware of the fact that the weather vane on the roof of the West Stand (in the form of a footballer) was modelled on George Hilsdon, so his memory lives on at Stamford Bridge.

HINTON, MARVIN. A fine central defender, who was not only powerful in the air but equally as dominant with the ball at his feet. Hinton was a footballer, not just a defender, he could pass, dribble, tackle, and shoot. Born in Norwood, South London, he first played for Charlton Athletic, signing professional in April 1957. He made 131 league appearances for the Valiants between 1957 and his move to Chelsea in August 1963. At Stamford Bridge his skills were nurtured and improved upon and he progressed to make 327 appearances for the Blues, scoring 3 goals. He won several honours with European clubs as well as domestic ones. Marvin Hinton was a genuinely nice man, a player who played with a smile upon his face and who was extremely good at what he did on the pitch, one of the best the club has ever had.

HITCHCOCK, KEVIN. Goalkeeper who is not blessed with the greatest height advantage. Kevin's career began with Nottingham Forest before he was signed by Mansfield Town in June 1984. He made some 182 league appearances for the Stags before Chelsea signed him in March 1988. Hitchcock is a good reflex-save keeper. At times he seems to have springs in his heels as he leaps all over the place protecting his goal. Like all keepers he is prone to the odd mistake but overall he is as good as any of the goalkeepers in the Premier League. A real joker in the pack, he has a quick and marvellous sense of humour, but when it comes to playing, his humour stays in the dressing room.

HODDLE, GLENN. England International with 53 full caps, and, as a player, one of the greatest midfielders of all time. His ball control and touch were at times unbelievable, his finishing was equally as astounding. His chipped goal in a game at Watford's Vicarage Road is one of the finest one could wish to see; skill and finishing of the highest order. Having moved abroad to play for Monaco he returned to the English game in 1991 with Swindon Town where he took over as player/ manager and led Swindon to promotion and incredibly into the Premier League. Such leadership and outstanding management did not go unnoticed and Hoddle was tempted

Glenn Hoddle

back to a big club; Chelsea. This infers no disrespect to
Swindon Town, but the potential at Chelsea was far greater
than it was at the County Ground, so he moved along the M4
in 1993 to become player/manager of the Blues. Since then he
has led Chelsea to an FA Cup final and into Europe as the club
look to the future. His laid-back style as a player is not evident
in Hoddle the manager, he is a man of high standards and he
expects the same of his players. It may well take a few years
yet, but Glenn Hoddle will lead Chelsea to greater things.

HOLLINS, JOHN. A Chelsea apprentice, John Hollins signed professional in July 1963 and spent 12 successful and happy years in the number 4 shirt deep in the heart of the first team. Hollins was a fighter, a never-say-die character whose commitment lasted the whole 90 minutes; he would be snapping like a terrier at the heels of forwards or defenders with as much tenacity in the last minutes of a game as in the first few minutes. Not only that, he could score goals too; 64 in his Chelsea career in two separate periods; July 1963–June 1975 and the 1983/84 season. In between he was just as inspirational at Queen's Park Rangers and Arsenal. It is incredible to believe that he made just one England full International appearance during his playing career. However, this never seriously concerned him, his job was with Chelsea and he did a good job.

In June 1985 he took over as manager of the club, a move which seemed quite natural as he had been coaching at the club and had passed on his considerable experience to those wishing to profit from his guidance. Unfortunately, things never quite worked out as well as they should have for Hollins the manager. A strict disciplinarian, he wanted players who wanted to play for Chelsea, not just earn a wage from the club, and this allegedly led to several confrontations with some of the so-called stars of the day. Of course, Hollins was right to want commitment, however team performances seemed to dip and this, accompanied by a press campaign to oust him, led to an air of uncertainty at the club. It seemed that the axe quivered above his head for many months and eventually it fell in March 1988 when the club went 4 months without a win! Hollins did his best, but in the end it was well short of what was required. Despite this he maintained an air of dignity about the whole affair, proving his self-discipline and earning him a great deal of respect from those journalists who had so maligned him as Chelsea manager.

HOPKIN, DAVID. Signed from Scottish club side Morton in September 1992, Hopkin is a midfielder-cum-striker. A hard-working player who will prosper under the watchful eye of Glenn Hoddle. He made his Chelsea debut at Anfield in February 1992 but has since found himself on the subs' bench for much of the time.

HOUSEMAN, PETER. Few can forget the silky skills of Peter Houseman running towards goal; with a deft flick to the left or right to put a colleague through on his own, or a pin-point accurate shot, he made the ball do the work. Signed in December 1962 he went on to make 324 appearances and score 39 goals. One which most will remember was in the 1970 FA Cup final when he exploited Leeds keeper Gary Sprake to the full. Knowing that Sprake was anything but reliable, Houseman speculatively hit a shot to Sprake's left from a distance of around 25 yards. The shot was not a powerful one, nor exquisitely accurate, it was a hit and hope effort which Sprake dived upon, fumbled and let in! Houseman raised both arms aloft in celebration, his intuition paid off. The goal ensured that Chelsea were back on level terms at 1–1 in the Wembley final. Ultimately, of course, after a 2–2 draw, the Blues won the replay 2–1, providing Houseman with some reward for his cunning effort. When transferred to Oxford in May 1975 at the age of 30 he still had much to offer the game. Indeed he was an inspiration at the Manor Ground where he made well over 60 appearances for the club before his career and life were brought to a drastic and sudden end in a fatal car crash in 1977. The memory of Peter Houseman will long be remembered by all Chelsea supporters who saw him play, his untimely death was a real loss to this marvellous game of ours.

HOUSTON, STEWART. Tall, lean defender whose playing career began at Stamford Bridge. Signed from Port Glasgow in August 1967 he made just 10 appearances for the Blues before a move to Brentford in March 1972. He later moved to Manchester United, Sheffield United and Colchester United and is currently running first-team affairs at Arsenal. His tactics as a player; to keep it simple and play the easy ball, worked wonders for him, providing him with a fine playing career. Houston was one who slipped through the Chelsea net.

HUDSON, ALAN. Quite simply, Alan Hudson was a genius with a football, a midfielder of outstanding quality and a terrace idol. I can still see him, long, flowing locks in feather-cut fashion, calmly taking the ball down in a game at Filbert Street, Leicester. Nonchalantly he placed his left foot on top of the ball and stood there for several seconds, seemingly unconcerned about the delay he was taking. Two Leicester players launched themselves towards him and Hudson, without a care in the world, rolled the ball back a few feet, turned his back on them and passed the ball to a colleague. The two Leicester players landed in a heap embarrassed and angry. Hudson turned to the crowd, smiled, winked, and took the return pass. It was delightful cheek, remarkable awareness and supreme skill. It was Alan Hudson.

He made 187 appearances for Chelsea, scoring 14 goals before a move to Stoke City in January 1974. He later moved to Arsenal, the United States, and then returned to Chelsea in August 1983. However, his stay at the Bridge second time round lasted just five months, before he moved back to Stoke City for a second time. He won 2 full England International caps in his career. Players of his sort are not evident in today's game, he had a rare quality and was a real crowd pleaser.

HUGHES, MARK. A remarkable capture by Glenn Hoddle. Hughes is a strong, rugged forward with a will to win, and never gives anything but total commitment. A Welsh full International, he first joined Manchester United as an apprentice making his first team debut in the 1983/84 season. There was a spell abroad, with Barcelona, and a loan spell with Bayern Munich before he returned to Old Trafford in 1988 where he has consistently scored 10-plus goals per season since, many being spectacular long-range volleys. Signed for Chelsea in July 1995 and will continue, I am certain, to score and thrill Chelsea fans week in week out.

HUGHES, THOMAS. Goalkeeper who spent much of his early career as understudy to the great Peter Bonetti and so was limited to just 11 first-team appearances between July

1965 and June 1971. A large and strong keeper he was, at times, a little slow at getting down to low shots. He transferred to Aston Villa in June 1971 and later played for Brighton and Hove Albion, and Hereford United.

HUMPHREYS, PERCY. Born in Cambridge in 1881, his playing career began with Cambridge St Mary's, before a move to London and Queen's Park Rangers, then Notts County in 1901. This was followed by a move to Leicester Fosse in June 1907. He arrived at Chelsea in February 1908 and was a capable and most competent inside-right, a real asset to a rapidly emerging Chelsea club. He had been capped at International level whilst at Notts County but failed to gain further honours in this field. Humphreys was the master of the dribble, he possessed great pace and could give the impression that the ball was permanently attached to his feet, as he set off on his high speed runs. Everything he did seemed to be at double-quick speed; he was tagged 'Headless Humphreys' because of this. All too often his speed of thought and movement would be so far ahead of his colleagues that his passing and interchanging would go astray. He moved to Tottenham Hotspur in December 1909, then back to Fosse in October 1911, before becoming player/manager of Hartlepool United in 1912.

HURST, GEOFFREY. Hurst, the player, is best known for scoring a hat-trick in the 1966 World Cup Final at Wembley. They say that all footballers are remembered for something and this outstanding feat is now firmly etched in all the record books. Hurst was a hungry goalscorer whilst playing with West Ham, his first professional club. He scored 6 goals in one game against Sunderland in an 8–2 victory and was reliable, with his strikes being on target in most games. He bagged 180 league goals for the Hammers, and a further 30 for Stoke when he moved there in 1972. Later, in 1975 he had a short spell in the West Midlands with West Bromwich Albion where 2 league goals were grabbed in 10 games. He joined Chelsea as first-team coach in 1979 and eventually took over as manager when Blanchflower stood down. It is surprising that although

Hurst's side played some terrific football, fast and freeflowing, they seemed unable to score enough goals to make them trophy winners. Try as he might, Hurst never solved the scoring problems and was relieved of his position in April 1981, much to the despair of many Chelsea supporters who enjoyed watching his team.

HUTCHINGS, CHRISTOPHER. Athletic full-back whose main asset was his strength. Hutchings liked nothing more than to make overlapping runs down the wing and to push himself forward. He was signed from Harrow Borough in July 1980 and went on to make 97 appearances and score 3 goals. He was sold to Brighton and Hove Albion in November 1983. Curiously, he had, in a previous match between the two clubs, been fined £250 for using insulting words to a police officer. Later he played for Huddersfield Town, Walsall and Rotherham United.

HUTCHINSON, IAN. Arrived from Cambridge United in July 1968, Ian Hutchinson was officially signed as a centre-forward but found himself playing alongside Peter Osgood who was more the central figure in the Chelsea attack. The pair worked well together, with Osgood feeding off Hutchinson's clever approach work. Good in the air and an astute passer of the ball Hutchinson's role was often overlooked in the Chelsea side of the late 1960s and early 1970s. His most appreciated moments came in the closing stages of the 1970 FA Cup final, when his glancing header foxed Leeds keeper Gary Sprake and earned Chelsea a replay. He was, however, more renowned for his tremendously long throw-in, he would arch his back to gain more momentum and launch the ball farther than many could kick it. This ploy created many goals. As a goalscorer himself, he netted 57 goals in 136 appearances and gained 2 England U23 International caps.

I

ILES, ROBERT. Goalkeeper signed from Weymouth in June 1978, Iles made 14 appearances between 1978 and 1982 but was never able to stake a serious claim to the number 1 jersey.

Tall and agile, he was not the most confident of goalkeepers in a Chelsea defence which was hardly inspiring.

INTERNATIONAL GAMES. England have played 4 full International games at Stamford Bridge:

5 April 1913	England 1 v Scotland 0
20 November 1929	England 6 v Wales 0
7 December 1932	England 4 v Austria 3
11 May 1946	England 4 v Switzerland 1

INTERNATIONALS. The following is a list of those players who, whilst on Chelsea's books, made full International appearances for their respective countries.

ENGLAND
K. Armstrong, 1, B.H. Baker, 1, D.J. Beasant, 2, R.T.F. Bentley, 12, F. Blunstone, 5, P.P. Bonetti, 7, P. Brabrook, 3,

B.J. Bridges, 4, J.G. Cock, 1, J.F. Crawford, 1, K.M. Dixon, 8, A.R. Dorigo, 6, J. Greaves, 15, J. Harrow, 2, G.R. Hilsdon, 8, J.W. Hollins, 1, T. Meehan, 1, G.R. Mills, 3, J.P. O'Dowd, 3, P.L. Osgood, 4, K.J. Shellito, 1, R.P. Sillett, 3, R. Spence, 2, R.V. Tambling, 3, T.F. Venables, 2, R.G. Wilkins, 24, J.E. Windridge, 8, D.F. Wise, 5, V.R. Woodley, 19, V.J. Woodward, 2.

NORTHERN IRELAND
J. Bambrick, 4, S.D. D'Aray, 2, W. Dickson, 9, M. Donaghy, 8, J. Ferris, 2, S.J. Irving, 2, J. Kirwan, 4, W. Mitchell, 11, T.J. Priestley, 1, K.J. Wilson, 30.

REPUBLIC OF IRELAND
A.G. Cascarino, 8, P.M. Mulligan, 11, R. Whittaker, 1.

SCOTLAND
T. Boyd, 2, P.S. Buchanan, 1, J. Cameron, 1, R. Campbell, 3, S. Clarke, 6, C. Cooke, 14, G.S. Durie, 11, R. Evans, 3, T. Law, 2, E.G. McCreadie, 23, D.R. Speedie, 5.

WALES
G.D. Hall, 9, T.J. Hewitt, 3, E. Jones, 2, J.P. Jones, 19, G. Moore, 3, P. Nicholas, 15, E.A. Niedzwiecki, 2, T.J.S. Phillips, 4, M. Thomas, 9.

IRVING, SAMUEL. International half-back signed from Cardiff City in 1929. Irving was a tough character and a tough player especially when challenging opponents for the ball. His passing up the field was occasionally a little wayward, but more often than not he found his man though perhaps not with the accuracy he would have wished. He gained 2 further International caps for Northern Ireland whilst with Chelsea, against England in 1929, and Wales in 1931 giving him a career total of 18. He previously played for Dundee before moving to Cardiff.

ISAAC, ROBERT. Bob Isaac was signed through the youth scheme where his play was confident and sensible. Isaac was a determined youngster who aimed to make it into the first team. He achieved this on 13 occasions, playing as a central defender. Yet, surrounded by players of some stature, many of whom played in his position, he was never likely to have an extended run in the first team. He was sold to Brighton and Hove Albion in February 1987 where he gained greater experience in the lower leagues. It was a great shame that this character could never maintain a level of consistency as he may well have progressed a good deal further.

J

JACKSON, ALEC. Outside-right who played for the club in the early 1930s. His playing career began in Scotland with Aberdeen, then moved to England, first with Huddersfield Town and then with Chelsea at Stamford Bridge in 1931. A Scottish International, he represented his country on 18 occasions. He scored a hat-trick for Scotland against England at Wembley in 1928.

JACKSON, JOHN. Scottish International goalkeeper signed from Partick Thistle in 1933. Jackson received a horrific injury in a game at Huddersfield Town, which left him hospitalised for three weeks, during which he lost his first-team place to Vic Woodley. Strangely, once recovered and languishing in the reserves, he was selected to play for Scotland, whilst Woodley was selected for England! Two International goalkeepers on the books at once! Jackson remained Chelsea's second choice to Woodley but continued to play for his country right up until 1936.

JASPER, DALE. Signed professional in January 1982, this midfielder-cum-defender was not particularly brilliant, but nevertheless was a clever footballer. His foresight with the ball at his feet was at times incredible as he made sweet upfield passes. The one area which required development was his tenacity and aggression when going into the tackle.

At times he waited that split second too long before going into a tackle thus conceding the advantage.

He transferred to Brighton and Hove Albion in May 1986 having made just 13 first-team outings and later played for Crewe Alexandria.

JOHNSEN, ERLAND. Strong central-defender signed from Bayern Munich in November 1989, Johnsen is a player who works hard and gives his all in every game. Good in the air and on the ground he is one of the best all-round players in the current side. A Norwegian International he has had no problems in adapting to the English-style game.

JOHNSON, GARY. Born in Peckham and signed professional in September 1977, Johnson had made some impact as a striker in local leagues. He made 18 first-team outings for Chelsea, scoring 9 goals before a move to Brentford in December 1980. Despite his fine goals per game ratio, Johnson never looked a likely International nor outstanding prospect. He later moved to South Africa and also appeared for Aldershot.

JOHNSTONE, DEREK. Scottish International striker signed from Glasgow Rangers in September 1983. Johnstone was one of several Rangers players making the transition from the Scottish to English game. Hardly made a great impact since he made just one first-team appearance. Later he played for Dundee United (on loan) and returned to Glasgow Rangers before a spell in management with Partick Thistle.

JONES, JOSEPH. Solid and determined defender, Joey Jones was a proverbial 'hard man' on the field of play. His career began at Wrexham before a move to Liverpool in July 1975 where he made 72 league appearances. Unfortunately his temperament was not what it should have been and he found himself targeted by the media and opposition fans for his tough and often rough tackling. A move back to Wrexham in October 1978 saw him curb his volatile nature and he proved his worth as a defender and team leader. It was this side of his game which influenced Chelsea to lure him to Stamford Bridge in October 1982. Sadly the tough side of his game re-emerged when he was sent off in a division 2 fixture at Carlisle. This aside, Jones was a hard worker in the Blues defence and his experience was passed onto the younger, less experienced players in the side, as Jones matured with the responsibility placed upon him. Eventually he moved to Huddersfield in August 1985 having made 85 appearances for Chelsea, and was called the 'Chopper' Harris of the 1980s, that is until the emergence of another cult figure with an identical surname as the Welshman.

JONES, KEITH. Midfielder who emerged through the ranks from the youth team. Jones possessed some marvellous attributes as midfielder; good judgment, vision, and bags of skill. Just where this disappeared to will remain a mystery, for the player had everything going for him, then, suddenly, after a spell out of the first team he lost it. In 57 appearances between 1983–1986 he scored 10 goals, but, having lost his confidence, it was felt that it would be in the interests of both club and player to allow him to leave. He moved to Brentford in September 1987 then on to Southend United in October 1991.

JONES, VINCENT. Vinny is a cult hero wherever he goes. An enigmatic, yet volatile character, he is, to the average football fan, everything they want in a player; amenable to fans' banter yet dedicated and committed in every tackle and move.

Vinny's career began at Wealdstone before a move to Wimbledon in November 1986. Here he attracted the attention of the media with his often reckless style of play, yet his rugged determination was praised. Jones was seen as an honest player who was a bit rough around the edges. A move to Leeds United in June 1989 was heralded as 'madness' by the press, yet United manager, Howard Wilkinson brought the best out of the player whose discipline record improved greatly whilst at Elland Road. Some 15 months later he was at Sheffield United, then came a move South, this time to Chelsea in August 1991. No one ever doubted his ability at Chelsea, the fans adored him and Vinny seemed to hold them in equal respect. In September 1992 the Blues sold him back to Wimbledon for a fee of £700,000 a healthy profit of £125,000 in just over twelve months.

Vinny Jones is very much more than just another footballer, he is a hero to thousands of fans from North and South, East to West and his minor indiscretions are laughed off as immature humour. His play is often maligned by soccer pundits but Vinny gives his all. How many players in today's game earn such nationwide respect? He made 52 appearances for Chelsea and scored 7 goals.

K

KEMBER, STEPHEN. Steve Kember was signed from Crystal Palace in September 1971. A skilful and well-presented footballer he possessed neat ball control and individual talent as a crowd pleaser. It was hoped that he would be another Alan Hudson, and Kember certainly had all the attributes to be as great as Hudson. With 3 England U23 appearances behind him, full International caps seemed certain to follow but they didn't. Kember's style of play became more determined and industrious, losing that occasional eccentricity which made him special. He had a terrific shot and often powered long-range efforts at unsuspecting keepers. In July 1975, having made 144 first-team appearances and plundered 15 goals he was sold to Leicester City. His Chelsea career had not been an inspired one, but Kember will always be remembered as a ball player. Later he moved back to Crystal Palace in October 1978.

KEVAN, DEREK. In a career which saw him appear for 8 individual league clubs spanning 15 years, Derek Kevan lasted just 5 months at Stamford Bridge. An inside-forward he was signed from West Bromwich Albion in March 1963 and made 7 appearances scoring one goal before being sold to Manchester City in August the same year. Kevan was a capable goalscorer and provider who made 14 full International appearances for England. He was a strong player whose power in the challenge earned him something of a 'clogger' tag. Such cynicism was not really warranted as he was a proven striker at all levels. He later played for Crystal Palace, Peterborough United, Luton Town and Stockport County.

KHAKI CUP FINAL. The 1915 FA Cup final was called the Khaki Cup final because of the high proportion of servicemen in attendance in their Khaki-coloured uniform. The game took place at Old Trafford, in Manchester, on 24 April 1915. An attendance of around 40,000 were present to witness Sheffield United beat Chelsea 3–0.

KHARIN, DIMITRI. Brilliant goalkeeper signed from CSKA Moscow for a fee of £200,000 in November 1982. Kharin has since proved to be a shrewd purchase since he has to be one of the best goalkeepers in the current Premier League. His agility and bravery has saved Chelsea on many occasions. A goalkeeper who inspires confidence in those in front of him and who will presumably be extremely difficult to dislodge from the number 1 jersey.

KIRKUP, JOSEPH. Full-back who hailed from Hexham in the North East of England. Joe was first signed by West Ham United in May 1957 where he made a solid, reliable reputation for himself in an 8-year spell at Upton Park. Arrived at Chelsea in March 1966 and continued to put in some excellent performances proving why he had been selected for England Youth and U23 caps earlier in his career. He made some 62 first-team appearances and scored 2 goals before his successful move to Southampton in February 1968 where he played his best football until 1973. Joe was a fine distributor of the ball; his head down, he would suddenly glance up and play off to a colleague before returning to position. Although somewhat mechanical he was very confident and very little got by him.

Dimitri Kharin

KITCHENER, RAYMOND. Outside-left signed from non-league side Hitchen Town in July 1954. Something of a nondescript type player, he found the step up to the highest grade of football a heavy burden. He made just one appearance for Chelsea before a move to Norwich City in September 1956.

KJELDBERG, JAKOB. Another overseas signing, Jakob Kjeldberg arrived at Stamford Bridge in a £400,000 deal from Silkeborg, Denmark. A defender-cum-midfielder he is a strong athletic player who is more than capable of holding his own in one-on-one defensive situations. A tough-tackling yet delightful ball player, he has the vision to play astute balls deep into the heart of the opposition's danger area thus creating opportunities for his own forwards. A player who has bridged the European gap settling into Premier League action with little or no problems. Many of the Chelsea faithful believe that he will show more consistency as he matures and excells in his role at the club. Signed in August 1993, I am sure that there is a lot more of Jakob that we have yet to see. Already with 60-plus appearances under his belt, he looks set for a bright future at the Bridge.

KNIGHTON, ALBERT. As a player he sustained an injury to his ankle which ended his playing career before it had really started. But, desperate to forge a career for himself in the game he loved so much, he turned to club management, beginning at Castleford Town in 1904. This was followed by spells at Huddersfield Town as assistant secretary, Manchester City as assistant secretary/manager, Arsenal as team manager, Bournemouth and Boscombe Athletic as team manager, Birmingham City as manager then Chelsea as team manager in August 1933. Under his command the club escaped relegation during his first season but went on to several mediocre campaigns. A quiet man, he concentrated on the first team and hardly ever got involved with training or coaching, leaving that to those with what he called 'more expertise'. He was an honest man and knew his capabilities in the field of management. At Chelsea he struggled to make any impression and it was no surprise that he left in April 1939, the beginning of the war years.

He later managed Shrewsbury Town and Portishead.

KNOX, THOMAS. Born in Glasgow and signed from East Stirling in June 1962, Knox was a flying outside-left whose crossing ability came into question during his 21 outings for the club. As a dribbler there was no doubting his class, he could leave defenders in his wake but sometimes he could lose the ball and simply retire from the chase. He was extremely frustrating for fans to watch mainly through his inconsistent form. This lead to his transfer to Newcastle United in February 1965, and he later appeared for Mansfield Town and Northampton Town.

L

LANGLEY, THOMAS. Born in Lambeth, London, Tommy Langley was one of the brightest young strikers to emerge through the Chelsea youth programme. Turning professional in April 1975, he made his first-team debut in the legendary number 9 shirt against Leicester City. His first league goal was scored in a 2–1 win over Birmingham City later in the 1974/75 season.

A robust striker, he quickly matured and became a regular first-teamer making some 139 appearances and scoring 43 goals between April 1975 and August 1980 when he moved to Queen's Park Rangers. Capped at England Schools, Youth and U21 levels, he went on to play for Crystal Palace, Coventry City, Wolverhampton Wanderers, Aldershot, AEK Athens and Exeter City, and also had a spell in Hong Kong.

LATE, ARRIVAL. On 27 December 1971 David Webb entered the pitch as first-team goalkeeper. Injuries had meant that the club were forced to bring in a reserve keeper in the form of Steve Sherwood. Sherwood, however, found himself stuck in traffic as he made his way to Stamford Bridge from Yorkshire.

Chelsea actually beat Ipswich Town on the day 2–0.

Webb's colleagues will tell you that he played his best ever game for the Blues that day!

LATE STARTERS. During the successful 1970 FA Cup campaign, Chelsea scored 20 of their 25 goal total in the second half of the competition; putting 4 past Crystal Palace, 4 past Queen's Park Rangers and 5 past Watford along the way.

LAVERICK, ROBERT. Left-winger who made 7 league appearances between 1955–1959. Laverick had shown much potential as a youngster and was actually drafted into the England Youth team. His lack of power seemed to hold him back, but his cheeky skipping runs could excite crowds who expected much of the youngster. Perhaps too much was expected of him, as his ability never materialised and a move took him to Everton in February 1959. Later he played for Brighton and Hove Albion, and Coventry City.

LAW, THOMAS. Player loyalty is something which has all but disappeared from the game as financial rewards are more eagerly sought than ties and associations with one team. Not so in the case of Tommy Law, modern day footballers take note, for Law remained at Chelsea all of his career. He was signed as a youngster from Glasgow Waverley and literally fell in love with Chelsea FC. As a full-back he was never outstanding but was very reliable and solid, so much so that he gained International recognition.

A cool and often relaxed footballer, Law enjoyed the pressure of the big game. Penalties were his speciality, few, if any, were missed and they accounted for the majority of his 19 goals scored. Law made 319 appearances for the Blues and turned down a big money move to French club Nimes who were going to treble his wage. There are those who will frown upon such a refusal but Law was happy with his lot, knowing full well that he would have to return one day, so why bother uprooting the family in the first place? Even when his playing days were over, Tommy could be seen down at the Bridge cheering the team on, and paying to get through the turnstiles!

LAWTON, THOMAS. Super striker and England International Tommy Lawton was known as one of the most prolific goalscorers of his era. He already had career totals of 16 league goals at Burnley, 60 at Everton, before he moved to Stamford Bridge in November 1945. He appeared in the league, for the Blues, on 42 occasions between his arrival and departure to Notts County two years later in November 1947. During that spell he scored 30 goals and was a real crowd favourite. His departure was received with great anger and uproar. Tommy was quick and strong, his lightning reflexes enabled him to perform at the highest level throughout an outstanding playing career.

Later he took up the post of player/manager at Brentford, before a move to Arsenal, then Kettering Town again as player/manager. He returned to Notts County as manager in May 1957, and went back again to Kettering Town in November 1963 where he was to become a club director. Finally he took up a coaching role with Notts County before retiring from the game.

LEADBETTER, JAMES. Signed as a fresh 21 year old from Edinburgh Thistle in July 1949, Jimmy Leadbetter struggled to get into the Chelsea first team. Indeed he made just 3 league appearances on the left wing before being released to Brighton and Hove Albion in August 1952 where he showed the consistent form which the Blues had hoped he would excite crowds with at Stamford Bridge. Later he played for Ipswich Town.

LEAGUE. Chelsea were accepted into the football league on Monday 29 May 1905, taking their place in the football league 2nd Division at the beginning of the 1906/07 season.

LEE, COLIN. Tall, lean player who was equally at home as a centre-half as he was as a centre-forward. Colin Lee was good in the air, a real fighter aided by great strength and a desire to be first. His playing career began with Bristol City before a brief loan spell at Hereford United sufficiently impressed his home town club, Torquay United, who signed him in January 1977. Just nine months later he was on his

101

way to London for Tottenham Hotspur where he was used in both midfield and attack. He signed for Chelsea in January 1980 and went on to make 200 appearances, scoring 41 goals before moving to Brentford in July 1987. Lee was a marvellous servant to Chelsea, his mature style and sensible game were applauded by most supporters, although it never quite inspired him to greater achievements, such as International recognition.

LEE, DAVID. Midfielder-cum-defender, David Lee is an athletic and determined player. Strong in the challenge he would push, shove, and harrass opposing players until he won the ball. The type of player all midfields require, gritty and constantly on the move, he has appeared for both England Youth and U21. Loan spells with Reading and Plymouth Argyle have provided him with greater experience of football outside the top flight. Perhaps some greater consistency will enhance his game and bring him greater honours.

Le SAUX, GRAHAM. Signed from St Paul's, Jersey, in December 1987, Graham Le Saux possessed a terrific left foot, his passing and crossing during his stay at Stamford Bridge were in a different class. Generally he played in a midfield/defensive role. He had pace not normally associated with someone of his build. A stockily-built individual he had the strength to hold off the challenge or to knock lesser players off possession.

During a turbulent last few games for the Blues he expressed a desire to leave, being dissatisfied with his role in the side. He got the move he wanted to big money spenders Blackburn Rovers in March 1993 in a player swap, with Steve Livingstone moving in the opposite direction!

He made 99 appearances for the Blues and scored 9 goals, he is now an established left-back at Blackburn and in the England International set up. During the 1980s and 1990s the Blues had two outstanding left-backs in the form of Dorigo and Le Saux, and it is a great shame neither could be tempted to stay. Curiously both went on to International recognition.

Graham Le Saux

LEWINGTON, RAYMOND. Midfielder, signed in February 1974 via the youth and apprenticeship set up. Lewington was a grafter, hard-working and unspectacular he proved himself to be a reliable character. It was to everyone's dismay that he never seemed to push himself to greater heights, being content to do what he was good at and never taking a gamble on the ball. After some 87 appearances and 4 goals, he moved from Chelsea to Vancouver Whitecaps, returning to England in 1979 and later playing for Wimbledon, Fulham (twice) and Sheffield United.

103

LIVESEY, CHARLES. Rambling centre-forward signed from Wolverhampton Wanderers in May 1959. Charlie was a typically old-fashioned-style striker. Strong, hard, and prepared to run until he dropped. His challenges were fair but tough, his shooting ability was at times wayward, but he held the basic theory that once you could see the goal, then you have a shot. This paid off as he scored 18 goals in 42 games before being sold to Gillingham in August 1961. Later he appeared for Watford, Northampton Town, and Brighton and Hove Albion.

LIVINGSTONE, STEPHEN. A tall and well-built centre-forward, Steve Livingstone was a hard-working if rather clumsy striker. His career began at Coventry City where he made a name for himself as a finisher. Such talent, any talent, was snapped up by Kenny Dalglish and Blackburn Rovers who hoped to nurture his rawness and turn him into quality. The result; they failed, and Livingstone was part of a swap deal which saw Graham Le Saux moved to Rovers. Hardly the greatest or most sensible transfer deal the club has ever made. Livingstone was a real let down, although committed and hard working he was never able to reproduce the quality or form for which Dalglish had signed him. He moved to Grimsby Town in 1993, where he immediately found his scoring boots. Everyone at Stamford Bridge was sad that the Livingstone move never worked out, he was a genuine and capable player who made only one appearance and scored no goals.

LLOYD, BARRY. England Youth International who played his football in the midfield. Signed at a time when the Blues were building a good defensive side, he found it hard to displace the likes of Hollins, Webb, and company. He made just 8 appearances before a good move to Fulham where his career blossomed. He played later for Hereford United, and Brentford.

LOCKE, GARY. Three hundred and fifteen appearances and 4 goals tells you all you need to know about this splendid right-back. Gary was an apprentice at the club and signed professional in July 1971 at the age of 17. An England Youth International, he was known as Mr Dependable by his Chelsea team-mates, as very few opposition players got anything out of him.

Reliable players do sometimes tend to appear anonymous in a good side, not so Locke, who pushed himself to the limit in every game. Having been at the club for over 11 years he was transferred to Crystal Palace in August 1990 when younger, fresh blood was emerging through the ranks. Many will thank 'Lockey' for passing on his vast experience, as he was always keen to help youngsters improve their game.

M

McALLISTER, KEVIN. Winger who signed from Scottish club side Falkirk in May 1985 and who was quick in thought as well as in pace, sometimes too quick, as his passes and crosses would go astray. He made 101 appearances scoring 13 goals between 1985–1990.

McANDREW, ANTHONY. Tall, powerful central midfielder, who made a name for himself at Middlesbrough gaining a solid and consistent reputation. McAndrew's game was not spectacular, he did the straight-forward things very well and knew his limitations. He signed for the Blues in September 1982 making just 23 appearances and scoring 4 goals before transferring back North to Ayresome Park in September 1984. He also played for Darlington and Hartlepool.

MACAULEY, JAMES. Tough wing-half who arrived from Edinburgh Thistle in October 1946. Jimmy possessed some fine, close ball control which he put to good use during his stay between 1946 and August 1951, when he was transferred to Aldershot. 'Wee Jimmy', as he was known, could certainly play; on the top of his form he was busy running off the ball and creating opportunities for his colleagues. He made 86 league appearances and scored 5 goals.

MacFARLAND, ALEX. Scottish inside-forward who joined Newcastle from Airdrieonians in October 1898 for a transfer fee of £30. He impressed at St James' Park but not so much as to make any real impact, so he returned to Scotland with Dundee in November 1901. Chelsea brought him South in 1913 but MacFarland was strangely out of sorts and could never match the form he had produced in Scotland. In fact he made only 4 first-team appearances for the Blues before he again returned to Scotland as manager of Dundee. In 1925 he returned to London to manage Charlton Athletic then in a strange merry-go-round of events he returned to Dundee as manager in 1927, and, yes, you guessed it, he returned to Charlton Athletic in May 1928. Eventually he left the Valley and took over as manager of Blackpool in 1933.

McCALLIOG, JAMES. Midfielder who progressed to a fine career in the game. Arrived from Leeds United, as an amateur in September 1963 and was drafted into the first team during the 1964/65 season. He made 12 appearances and scored 3 goals before a sizeable transfer fee move to Sheffield Wednesday. He made 5 full International appearances for Scotland having gained honours at School and U23 levels. Later he played for Wolverhampton Wanderers, Manchester United, Southampton and Lincoln City.

McCREADIE, EDWARD. Born in Glasgow in 1940, Eddie McCreadie developed into one of the best full-backs Chelsea have ever had. Signed for the club in April 1962 from East Stirling, having been under the watchful eye of Tommy Docherty for some time, he now seems a bargain at just £6,000. Eddie was best at left full-back where his astute sliding tackles broke down dozens of dangerous assaults upon the Chelsea goal. However, he is best remembered for scoring the winning goal, playing at centre-forward, in the 1965 League Cup final where he ran virtually from one end of the pitch to the other before netting the all-important strike. Eddie still smiles about it to this day when you mention it to him.

Scottish International recognition in the form of 23 full caps was just reward for his talents. When his playing days were finished it was a common belief that he would one day become team manager. This happened in April 1975 when he took over a struggling side and totally rebuilt and transformed them, however behind the scenes all was not well, although his young side won promotion back to the 1st division he believed that he did not have the full support of the board and left in July 1977. In a career total of 405 appearances he scored 5 goals, none more important than his League Cup final effort.

McFARLANE, IAN. Ian McFarlane was a well-built full-back who worked hard at his game and fitness and was a credit to every club be served, both as a player and a manager. His career began with Aberdeen in 1955 before Chelsea signed him in August 1956. At Stamford Bridge he made 43 appearances before Leicester City paid £9,000 for his services in May 1958. After a spell with Bath City he moved to Middlesbrough as assistant manager, then Manchester City, before Carlisle United gave him his chance to prove himself as team manager in 1970. McFarlane was a hard task master, yet got the best out of his troops; at Carlisle he signed the wayward Stan Bowles and taught him some self-discipline which served him well in his future career. Results never went well in Cumberland and McFarlane walked out of Brunton Park. Later he moved to Sunderland as assistant and caretaker manager and then Leicester City. He worked as chief scout for Leeds United until 1995 when he finally retired from the game he has served so well.

McINNES, JOHN. Inside-forward who arrived from Morton, in Scotland, where he had been outstanding as a youngster. Neat passing movements seemed to bounce off him like a bouncing ball. Quick-footed and adaptable he made 37 league appearances for the Blues, and scored 5 goals between 1946–1949.

McKENZIE, DUNCAN. Extrovert striker who had made several big-money moves to clubs such as Leeds United, Anderlecht, and Everton, so there was no doubting his credentials when he arrived in London with Chelsea in September 1978. Unfortunately Chelsea were not to see the best of his goalscoring prowess after only 16 games and 4 goals, he moved to Blackburn Rovers within six months, preferring life and football in the North of England.

McKNIGHT, PHILLIP. Wing-half signed just after the Second World War in January 1947 from Alloa Athletic. McKnight was tough, as one would expect from a player in such a position, however his passing was weak and he lacked flair and ingenuity in the middle of the field. He made 33 league appearances scoring only one goal before a move to Leyton Orient in July 1954.

McLAUGHLIN, JOSEPH. Central defender, Joe was a real character in the Chelsea squad. He was a terrific climber when called upon for aerial combat, either in defence or in attack. On many occasions he outjumped opposing players giving the impression that the other player hadn't jumped at all. On the ground he was cool and rather sophisticated for a player of his sort, and was more than proficient at dribbling his way forward and laying off the odd cultured pass. In a Chelsea career that saw him make 268 appearances and score 7 goals, Joe also received Scottish U21 recognition with 10 caps.

He remained at the club between June 1993 and August 1989 when he moved to Charlton Athletic and later played for Watford. He is currently playing for Falkirk in Scotland.

McMILLAN, ERIC. McMillan hailed from Yorkshire and signed for the club in April 1958. He returned to his native county in July 1960 with Hull City and later played for Halifax Town. He made 5 goalless league appearances for Chelsea.

McNALLY, ERROL. Goalkeeper, signed from Portadown in December 1961, who proved himself to be of an acceptable standard but who was mainly restricted to the reserves where he put in many fine performances. He played a career total of 9 league games for Chelsea between 1961–1963 before returning to Ireland.

McNEIL, ROBERT. Left-winger signed from Scottish side Hamilton Academicals in 1914. McNeil was dynamite, a sweet dribbler and fine striker of the ball. According to legend, he was also dynamite in the dressing room, full of quips and jokes maintaining a high morale.

McNICHOL, JOHN. An inside-forward who failed to make the grade with Newcastle United and who found himself playing on the South coast with Brighton and Hove Albion.

Signed for Chelsea in August 1952 and made an instant impact with his neat play and passing on the edge of the penalty box. Goals were no problem with some 60 league strikes notched up in 181 appearances between 1952–1957. McNichol was one of a kind, so much so that he became the mainstay of the team which was built around him. He moved to Crystal Palace in March 1958.

McROBERTS, ROBERT. Bobby McRoberts, as you can probably guess, was born in Scotland. At the age of 18 he was turning out for his local side, Coatbridge. Then followed moves to Airdrieonians and Albion Rovers. He then moved to England with Gainsborough Trinity in 1896, before a move to Small Heath in 1898 for a fee of £150. Chelsea signed him in August 1902 for £100 as an investment for the future, with football league status being the club's ultimate aim. Of course, this came just three years later, and McRoberts was part of that first ever league season. He made 114 appearances for Chelsea and took over as team captain in 1907. A player who could interchange between centre-forward or centre-half, he was equally at home in either role. He went on to manage Birmingham City in 1910.

MALCOLM, ANDREW. Another battling defender who was signed from fellow London side, West Ham United in November 1961. Unfortunately for Malcolm, although his ambition was admirable he was not equal to the players Chelsea were bringing into the club. He made 27 league appearances in the 1961/62 season without ever being outstanding. His Chelsea career total stands at 28 games and one goal, before a move to Queen's Park Rangers. Many felt that he had too much of the West Ham game in him to fit into the Chelsea style.

MANAGERS. A full list of Chelsea's managers since 1905 makes impressive reading, with some of the game's greatest footballers having held the reigns at Stamford Bridge:

April 1905 – October 1906 John Tait Robertson
August 1907 – June 1933 David Calderhead Snr
August 1933 – April 1939 Leslie Knighton
May 1939 – May 1952 Billy Birrell
June 1952 – September 1961 Ted Drake
October 1961 – October 1967 Tommy Docherty
October 1967 – October 1974 Dave Sexton
October 1974 – April 1975 Ron Suart
April 1975 – July 1977 Eddie McCreadie
July 1977 – December 1978 Ken Shellito
December 1978 – September 1979 Danny Blanchflower
September 1979 – April 1981 Geoff Hurst
May 1981 – June 1985 John Neal
June 1985 – March 1988 John Hollins
March 1988 – May 1991 Bobby Campbell
June 1991 – February 1993 Ian Porterfield
March 1993 – to date Glenn Hoddle

MANAGER. The longest-serving manager has been David Calderhead at 25 years and 10 months. The manager who kept his job for the least time was Ron Suart with just six months in charge. Curiously no less than 7 managers have lasted less than two years in the post, which is odd, as Chelsea had just 7 managers in their first 58 seasons in the league, then 10 in the following 21 seasons!

MANAGER—SUCCESS. The most successful team manager has been Tommy Docherty, followed by David

Glenn Hoddle the Manager

Sexton, David Calderhead, then John Neal, Bobby Campbell and Ted Drake.

MATTHEW, DAMIAN. Born in Islington, Damian was a revelation in the youth leagues. Outstanding performances in midfield attracted Chelsea who signed him in June 1989. He went on to make 19 appearances for the club, and spent a loan spell with Luton Town. He was signed by Crystal Palace in February 1994 for a fee of £125,000 and has made 9 England U21 appearances to date.

MATTHEW, REGINALD. England International goalkeeper signed from Coventry City in November 1956. Courageous and defiant, he was a striking figure between the posts. Few goalkeepers could read the game as well as he and his concentration for the 90 minutes hardly ever

113

diminished. He moved to Derby County in October 1961 having made 148 appearances for Chelsea.

MAYBANK, EDWARD. Teddy Maybank was another apprentice who came good. A forward, he managed to break into the first team in 1974 making his debut against Tottenham Hotspur. He went on to make 32 appearances for the club and scored 6 goals before Fulham managed to prize him away from Stamford Bridge in November 1976. Later he played for Brighton and Hove Albion before returning to Fulham. Teddy was sharp, but not quite the finisher everyone had hoped he would be. He forged a good career for himself and found the target more regularly once he'd moved away from Stamford Bridge.

MAYES, ALAN. Prolific, but not quick, Alan Mayes was lethal in front of goal in a career which saw him play for Queen's Park Rangers, Watford, Northampton Town and Swindon Town before Chelsea. He netted 14 goals in 72 games and was influential in many other goals for his fellow strikers. Mayes was hardly the tallest of players but you could guarantee he would give it everything he had. His spell at Chelsea was brief, December 1980 to July 1983, but it was sufficient for him to prove his worth. He also played for Carlisle United, Newport County and Blackpool.

MEEHAN, THOMAS. Born in Manchester in 1896, Tommy Meehan was a slightly-built footballer, standing at just 5′ 5″ in his stocking feet and weighing around 9½ stones he had to rely on skill to see him through rather than physique. His career began in local football with Newtown, Walkden Central before a major step up to Rochdale in 1916. Meehan was a busy player who could attack as well as defend. These qualities encouraged Manchester United to take him on in 1917. At Old Trafford he continued to shine, passing and running off the ball and encouraging others to do the same. In 1920 came a move away from Manchester, to the bright lights of London, with Chelsea. It was a marvellous signing by the club, attracting such an outstanding talent. Meehan shone like a bright lantern on the darkest night, his play was clean and attractive. In 1924 he gained his sole full International cap with England with the 0–0 draw with Northern Ireland in Belfast. Sadly, it was to be his last cap, as he was cruelly struck down with polio and died whilst at the very height of his career. Football can be a cruel game, but life can be far worse.

MILLAR, JOHN. Scottish defender signed in August 1984 and who broke into the first team during the 1985/86 season making 11 appearances. He never really established himself in the side and was transferred to Blackburn Rovers after a loan spell with Northampton Town in 1987. At Ewood Park his career took a more consistent manner with over 122 league appearances for Rovers.

MILLER, JAMES. The club's first ever trainer and strict disciplinarian worked the players hard. Miller died in Christmas 1906, and his passing was greatly mourned by the Chelsea players, the majority of whom held him in the highest regard.

MILLINGTON, SIMEON. This goalkeeper, signed from non-league football in Shropshire, was a tall and calm man who never seemed flustered. He signed at the beginning of the 1926/27 season and was first choice until his forced retirement from the game, in 1932, when a back injury became too much for him to bear. He was better known as Sam Millington.

MILLS, GEORGE. A large centre-forward who scored on his first-team debut against Preston North End on 21 December 1929. Mills remained part of the Chelsea set up for several years to come, plundering goals almost at his will. His nickname 'The Bomb' is an apt description of his style of play. He retired from the game whilst with Chelsea during the war. His previous clubs included Emerald Athletic, and Bromley. He won 3 full England International caps in 1938.

MITCHELL, DAVID. Striker who gained invaluable experience overseas with Feyenoord before signing for Chelsea in December 1988. Davey Mitchell was an aggressive striker. Tall and lean he could be seen tugging at the sleeves of defenders in possession. He made only 8 appearances for Chelsea finding the transition from Holland rather difficult and, after a brief loan spell with Newcastle, he found himself at Swindon Town in July 1991, where he used his experience and skill to their benefit.

MITCHELL, FRANK. A defender, his playing days began at Coventry City where he was an amateur with a bright future. Signed by Birmingham City in September 1943 he remained at St Andrews until January 1949 when Chelsea stepped in for his services. Mitchell was a leader in the defence with his no-nonsense tackling and robust clearances. Hoofing the ball clear at the merest hint of danger was hardly attractive, but very effective. He made some 75 league appearances for Chelsea and scored one goal before a move to Watford in August 1952.

MOLYNEUX, JAMES. Fine goalkeeper who graced the Chelsea goal for several seasons mainly between 1912 and 1916, including in an FA Cup final appearance in 1915, when, sadly, he conceded 3 goals in a bad defeat.

MOORE, GRAHAM. Midfielder whose talents were vastly underrated during his time at Stamford Bridge. Moore had signed from Cardiff City in December 1961 for a then club record fee of £35,000. Although signed as a goalscorer, 14 goals in 72 appearances is not a great return. However, Moore possessed other skills which made him an asset to the team, a target man, he could hold up the ball and lay it off.

He could also flick on neat headers and turn his defender. For a cumbersome-looking man he could turn on a sixpence. Sadly, it was goals he was shy of, and he was sold to Manchester United in November 1963 where he again failed to deliver. He also played for Northampton Town, Charlton Athletic and Doncaster Rovers.

MONKOU, KENNETH. Signed from Feyenoord, Holland, in March 1989, this hulk of a man, who played as a central defender, looked ineffective and clumsy. How wrong first impressions can be, Monkou turned out to be a first-rate defender. Fair yet tough, he was not frightened to put his head where others wouldn't. He played 117 games and scored 2 goals before a move to Southampton in August 1992. Monkou was a pillar in the Chelsea defence and is playing a similar role at the Dell where Alan Ball has arranged his defence around him.

MORTIMORE, JOHN. Born in Hampshire, 'Morti' stood tall and firm in the heart of the Chelsea defence for almost 8 years. As an aerial powerhouse he was the best; hustling and bustling, he won just about everything that travelled above six feet in the air during a game. Signed from non-league side, Woking, in April 1956 and made 279 appearances scoring only 10 goals, few for such a dominant player. Yet, Mortimore knew his place was in defence and this is where he played his heart out. At the age of 31, in September 1965, he was transferred to Queen's Park Rangers, but he much preferred the atmosphere of the Bridge on a matchday.

MULHOLLAND, JAMES. Forward who never quite made it whilst at the club. Jamie was signed from Scottish club, East Stirling. Neat and quick, he flattered to deceive as defenders could read his game and outwit him easily. Despite this he bagged 3 goals in 12 games for the Blues. He was sold to Morton and later returned to England with Barrow, Stockport County and Crewe Alexandria. He was with Chelsea from 1962–1963.

MULLIGAN, PATRICK. Paddy Mulligan was a favourite with the fans. A Republic of Ireland International, he went on to achieve a career total of 51 caps for his country, no mean feat for any player. Mulligan was signed from Shamrock Rovers in October 1969. He became an instant hit as he smiled and talked to fans before, during and after games. As a footballer he was reliable and not overly arrogant, but just enough to antagonise opposing forwards. Paddy could often get himself involved in heated situations but would come out smiling and shaking hands with his opponent. He made 73 appearances and scored 2 goals for Chelsea. He later moved to Crystal Palace in September 1972. He also played for West Bromwich Albion.

MURPHY, JEREMY. Midfielder signed from Crystal Palace in August 1985. Murphy never really found form at Stamford Bridge despite appearing as an International with the Republic of Ireland. After 39 appearances and 3 goals, a loss of form coincided with some niggling injuries which caused him to lose his place in the first team.

MURRAY, ALBERT. Winger, and England schools, youth and U23 player, who had an amazing burst of pace which could propel him down the right wing and into dangerous positions. Bert was a product of the Chelsea youth squad and was a star wherever he went. He charmed crowds with his cute first touch and cheeky sorties, beating defenders, once, twice, sometimes three times. He was supremely arrogant with the ball at his feet. He made 179 appearances for the first team between May 1961 and August 1966 when he transferred to Birmingham City. Murray also appeared for Brighton and Hove Albion and Peterborough United.

N

NEAL, JOHN. Team manager between May 1981 and June 1985, John Neal had previously managed Wrexham and Middlesbrough before arriving at Stamford Bridge in May 1981, replacing Geoff Hurst. At the time it was not a popular move by the Chelsea board, as fans clamoured for an ex-player to take the helm, with John Hollins being the obvious selection. The board resisted the fans' pressure, a move which was to work in their favour. John Neal had many contacts within the game, and at once declared that Chelsea was not a club which should be languishing in the second division. It was his intention to take them back to the top flight. This was a positive statement, typical of every new manager taking over a club, the difference on this occasion being that Neal meant it! He set about assessing every player in the squad, and monitored practice and training matches. Before long he had changed the side around, moving players into new roles which they seemed to relish. In 1983 he signed 7 new players, releasing those with no future at the club – it was a huge gamble. Chelsea had just escaped relegation the previous season. Neal knew what he was doing. The Blues took the 2nd division by storm that 1983/84 season, winning the Championship on goal difference above Sheffield Wednesday. Chelsea were back in the 1st division, Neil had kept his promise. The pressures of the job had been getting to Neal, his health had clearly been suffering during that vital campaign, and in the summer he underwent heart surgery, but was back, ready and waiting for the new season. The first season back in the top flight was a reasonably good one, as Chelsea finished the league in 6th position. It was now that the Chelsea board gave the fans their previous wish and in came John Hollins to replace Neal. The move was agreed by all parties and was seen as being in John Neal's best interests. The supremo took a place on the Chelsea board, but missed the positive adrenalin buzz of the managerial role and so stood down from his elevated position. Basically, he sorely missed the day-to-day activities of team management; the worry, the stress, the pressures were what kept him interested in the game. Unfortunately, the exciting style Neal had introduced into the team seemed to disappear under Hollins' reign, injuries causing the new manager real grief. For a man whom the fans initially did not want, John Neal became one of the most respected managers the club has ever had. Every Chelsea supporter who maligned the club upon his arrival, had to admit that they were wrong, and it was a great pity that his health had suffered, as John Neal would undoubtedly have taken the club on to greater achievements.

NEKREWS, THOMAS. Central defender from Chatham, Kent. Tommy Nekrews was a trialist whose initial promise was never quite realised at Stamford Bridge. An excellent header of the ball he was signed as an amateur from local soccer. He never appeared for the first team and moved to Gillingham in September 1953.

NELMES, ALAN. A promising youngster who signed for the club in October 1965. Despite desperate efforts to break into the Chelsea team he never sufficiently proved himself. He could be slow to read the game, which, as a defender, is not an ideal trait. He moved to Brentford in July 1967 where he became a regular in the first team for over 7 seasons.

NEVIN, PATRICK. Glaswegian winger who first played for Clyde in the Scottish league. Nevin was brought to Chelsea by John Neal in July 1983 and was an instant success. A Scotland full International, Nevin also won honours in the Youth and U21 sides, as well as Scotland 'B'.

Few modern players could excite a crowd as Pat so often did. With a fantastic turn of pace, his slight frame would flee down the right wing in a style reminiscent of Billy Whizz. This was not the winger's only fine attribute, as Nevin could pass and cross the ball as well as anyone in the league. One reporter of the mid-1980s declared that Nevin was the

Pat Nevin

modern-day Stanley Matthews; praise indeed, but hardly accurate. Although he could be outstanding, there were times when he seemed to lack the confidence to go past his man. The skill he had shown in previous games virtually disappeared for the whole 90 minutes in some games. Inconsistency began to creep into his game, though whether this was due to a slump in the team's form, or whether it was time for a move we shall never know. But move, Pat Nevin did.

After 237 appearances and 45 goals, Pat was sold to Everton in July 1988 and now plays his football for Tranmere Rovers where he is one of the stars of the team. Any inconsistency in his game has vanished as he has matured into a fine player. Even though his pace has diminished somewhat, he still possesses an intelligent football brain which is used to maximum effect in each game. Nevin will remain a firm favourite with the Chelsea fans: while not too many players can claim to have earned the respect of the Blues support, Pat is one who can.

NEWTON, EDWARD. Strong and athletic midfielder Eddie Newton has proved himself to be a capable player and keen motivator as well as a real workhorse in the heart of the Chelsea team. He is a useful addition to the Blues attack and supports his front runners well. Signed from the youth side in May 1990 the player has been a real success story, proving the quality and effectiveness of the Youth scheme. A spell on loan with Cardiff City in January 1992 was thought to be of use to Newton and the club, providing invaluable experience. He made 18 league appearances for the Bluebirds and scored 4 goals. He has made International appearances for England at Youth and U21 level. If his progress continues, then full International honours will be a distinct possibility.

NICHOLAS, ANTHONY. Born in East London, Nicholas was attracted to Chelsea as a youth and eventually signed for the club in May 1955. A strong and pacey forward, his agility and quick feet often caused havoc in the opposition's penalty area. Good on the run with the ball at his feet, he

Eddie Newton

scored a memorable goal on 21 September 1957, in the 6–1 demolition of Burnley at Stamford Bridge. Everyone in the ground gave Nicholas a standing ovation as he turned to celebrate his piece of magic, leaving the Burnley players somewhat bemused by his trickery on the ball.

Sadly this was Tony's best performance in a blue shirt; on occasions his play was, quite frankly, indifferent. The undoubted talent he possessed could never be harnessed. So inconsistent was his performance that he could never hold down a regular first-team place which was frustrating for the management as the fans were aware of his ability and often questioned manager Ted Drake's awareness. Eventually, in November 1960, Nicholas was sold to Brighton and Hove Albion before dropping into the non-league game with Chelmsford City. Although there was a brief return to the professional game with Leyton Orient, he never truly performed consistently for anyone. He made a total of 63 appearances for the Blues and scored 20 goals.

NICHOLAS, PETER. Welsh International midfielder signed from Aberdeen in August 1988, Peter Nicholas was a combative and crafty midfielder, who scored 2 goals in 92 appearances for Chelsea between 1988 and 1991 when he transferred to Watford. Signed by Crystal Palace as a youngster in December 1976, he made International appearances at schools and U21 levels and was soon turning in some excellent performances in the Palace first team. One hundred and twenty seven league appearances later he was signed by Arsenal in March 1981 but struggled to make any real impact at Highbury and seemed unsettled. Palace came to his rescue in October 1983 bringing him back to Selhurst Park. Nicholas had two educated feet and was an expert at the long ball pass, perfectly weighting such balls for the use of his front men. Luton Town prised him away from Palace in January 1985 before his move to Aberdeen a couple of seasons later. At Chelsea he was a gritty and determined player, prone to the odd lunging tackle which would often get him into trouble with match officials. Such was his style that he was classed as one of the tough men of the team. Although his skill was, at times, breathtaking, as he could take control of the ball and juggle it about before passing it out wide with superb vision. He moved to Watford in March 1991 having made 92 appearances and banged in 2 goals!

NICKNAME. The club's official nickname has altered through the years. Originally 'The Pensioners' as in the Chelsea pensioners, war veterans, this was later dropped for obvious reasons. Chelsea are now more commonly known as 'The Blues'.

NIEDZWIECKI, EDWARD. Tall and solid goalkeeper, the Welsh-born Niedzwiecki first played for Wrexham, signing for the club in July 1976. He had turned in several performances for the Welsh Schoolboys which had attracted a number of clubs, but Wrexham were quick to get his signature, the stay in Wales presumably suiting him more than a move away from home. For a long time, Niedzwiecki did not seem to be going anywhere, as he turned in reliable performances with some consistency. He was, as all goalkeepers can be, anonymous, with the outfield players taking much of the glory in victories and outstanding games. The reality was a little different as Eddie kept the team motivated with his solid displays, instilling confidence in his back four.

Chelsea took him on board in June 1983. In desperate need of a quality goalkeeper, the Blues had never found an ideal replacement for Peter Bonetti, and they bought Eddie whose tall frame dominated the Chelsea goalmouth. Good with crosses, a pleasant change for a Chelsea keeper, his bravery and agility were a source of inspiration. Like many a large goalie, he could be a little slow to get down to the low shot, but such errors were few and far between. He made a total of 175 appearances in the Chelsea goal between 1983 and 1987.

NUTTON, MICHAEL. Born in London, Mike Nutton played his early football as a Chelsea apprentice. A central-defender he was powerful and determined, but often a little reckless. He lacked aerial ability but was strong enough to take control of most situations. His pace was of real advantage in sprinting challenges for control of the ball. He made 81 appearances for the Blues between 1977 and March 1983 when he joined Millwall. In between he enjoyed a loan spell at Reading in February 1983, with 6 appearances for the Elm Park club.

O

OAKTON, ERIC. Speedy, diminutive winger signed from Bristol Rovers at the beginning of the 1932/33 season. An experienced player, he added that little extra width to the side in his all too brief spell with the club. A good crosser of the ball, he was an expert at taking full-backs down to the corner flag, and dribbling past them, leaving them behind as he broke towards goal.

O'CONNELL, SEAMUS. Born in Carlisle, Cumberland, he first signed for Scottish club side, Queen's Park. O'Connell was a fast and efficient inside-forward. His speed and quick thinking caused defenders all kinds of problems as he buzzed about the pitch. He moved to Middlesbrough as an amateur in May 1953 and continued to work hard for himself and his colleagues. His face did not seem to fit at Ayresome Park which is why he was turning out for Bishop Auckland when Chelsea snaffled him up in August 1954.

He was a real sensation when he first arrived, as the Blues fans had never before seen such a busy player, with a lovely touch and a keen eye for the half-chance. Seamus was a clever finisher and scored 12 goals in 17 games for the club. He returned to the North of England in 1956 before signing for his beloved Carlisle United in February 1958.

O'DOWD, PETER. A huge centre-half whose dominance in the air was second to none. He was self-reliant and depended on no-one, playing his own game and keeping things simple. His Chelsea debut was a torrid one, against Everton and the mighty Dixie Deans. The Toffeemen ran out 7–2 winners, with Deans bagging 5. It was O'Dowd who was given the task of marking him on the day. However, he could not be wholly blamed for the result as the Everton side were inspired.

O'Dowd, an England International with 3 full caps, against Scotland in 1932, and Northern Ireland and Switzerland in 1933, began his football career with Apperley Bridge. He later moved to Selby Town and Blackburn Rovers as an amateur before turning professional with the club in December 1926. A move to Burnley followed in March 1930 before Chelsea came in for him in November 1931. O'Dowd was nothing spectacular, but few players have been as reliable in the central-defender's role. He moved from Chelsea and adapted to the European game with Valenciennes of France in September 1935. He finally returned to England at the age of 29, signing for Torquay United in March 1937, where he cruelly broke his leg in a trial game and was forced to retire from the game. He died on 8 May 1964, aged just 56. This honest Yorkshireman must rank as one of the best centre-halfs the club has ever had.

ORD, THOMAS. Ex-Erith and Belvedere striker, Ord was a star in the local league. His 'feather-cut' hairstyle and neatly-trimmed beard gave him an older appearance than his play suggested. Signed by Chelsea in December 1972 he made just 3 first-team appearances and scored on his debut at home to Stoke City on 7 April 1973; unfortunately it was in a 3–1 defeat. He was loaned later to Bristol City but never actually turned out for them. Ord was tempted by the glamour and ritz of the game in the United States so he took his talents over there the following season, and played for Montreal Olympic, Rochester Lancers, New York Cosmos, Vancouver Whitecaps, Seattle Sounders, Tulsa Roughnecks and Atlanta Chiefs. Ord was a nice lad but at Chelsea he was a little fish in a big pond and he was unlikely to become anything else in the English game, hence his move.

O'ROURKE, JOHN. Born in Northampton, John O'Rourke was an elegant and prolific goalscorer late on in his career. His career began as an amateur with Arsenal where he performed with some considerable quality. With a powerful heading ability and a vicious shot he was a clear candidate for further glories. He signed for Chelsea in April 1962 but managed just one game for the Blues, learning his trade in the reserves. In December 1963 he moved to Luton Town, where his career really took off. He later played for Middlesbrough, Ipswich Town, Coventry City, Queen's Park Rangers and Bournemouth. He gained International honours as a schoolboy and at U23 level for England.

OSGOOD, PETER. Terrific, tall, lean and elegant centre-forward, Ossie was excellent in the air and equally as deadly on the ground. Having signed from the junior ranks, where he was prolific, he progressed through to the first-team ranks, signing professional forms in September 1964, where he matured sufficiently to warrant a place in the first eleven. As he scored goal after goal, he became one of the most wanted centre-forwards in the English game, but this quietly spoken Southerner, who hailed from Windsor, was happy with his lot at Chelsea. He was surrounded by players of the same age and it was clear that if the side could stay together then there was real potential for honour and glory. The Chelsea side was filled at the time with such talent as Ron Harris, Eddie McCreadie, John Hollins, Ian Hutchinson, Peter Houseman and Charlie Cooke. Ossie was an integral part of this lot. By 1970, the club were beginning to fire on all cylinders; Cooke and Houseman were able providers for the head of Osgood who also appeared to be able to read Ian Hutchinson's mind. He scored a terrific goal in the FA Cup final replay against Leeds at Old Trafford, when he finished off a fine move by throwing himself onto a diving header which left Leeds keeper, David Harvey, with no chance and equalised, bringing Chelsea back into the game. Then there was the marvellous solo performance against Arsenal, when he dominated in the air, flicking balls off left, right and centre, before volleying a superb goal into the back of the net, all without the ball touching the ground! A full England International, with 4 caps, he also gained honours at Youth and U23 level for his country. Ossie meant a great deal to the average Chelsea fan. His loyalty in remaining at the club when he could have left in his prime was regarded as a sign of great allegiance. Ossie was a hero, furthermore, he was a hero who would never let the club down.

In March 1974, after almost 10 full years at the Bridge, he was sold to Southampton where he continued to plunder goals. A brief loan spell at Norwich in 1976 was followed by a move to the United States of America, with Philadelphia. Then in December 1978, Ossie came home, returning to Chelsea, but by now, his playing days were all but over, he made only a further 11 appearances and scored 2 goals before calling it a day. In a Chelsea career total of 375 appearances, he scored 150 goals! Five of these were netted in one game against Jeunesse Hautcharage in 1971; in total he scored 8 goals against this club in two games.

OXBERRY, JOHN. Appointed as first-team trainer by Ted Drake at the beginning of the 1952/53 season. Oxberry had previously worked for Drake at Reading and both held the other in great respect. Indeed, Drake gave much credit to his right-hand man, whom he trusted implicitly.

P

PARSONS, ERIC. Right-winger who was signed from West Ham United in December 1950. He made 2 appearances as an England 'B' International which possibly speaks volumes for this player. When he joined the club he fell foul to a particularly nasty cartilage injury which kept him out of the game for a short while. The Chelsea faithful felt cheated believing that West Ham had conned the club in their purchase of the player. There were incredible scenes when he appeared in the stand at one game with some of the crowd quite clearly against him. Eric, though, was a good-natured lad and kept calm throughout this turmoil. When he did get back to full fitness it was a very different story, as he soon became a star of the team, and a real crowd pleaser. Fickleness has always been associated with football supporters! A fine exponent of taking on defenders and running at defences in general, Parsons could dance his way around and through the best, although on occasion he would go a little too far, when an early ball to a colleague might have created a better opportunity. He made a total of 158 league appearances for Chelsea, and scored 37 goals between 1950 and November 1956 when he moved to Brentford.

PATES, COLIN. England Youth International central defender, Pates graduated from the Chelsea youth set up, into the first eleven and was, in some games, a revelation. Born in Carshalton, London, he had shown great promise at schoolboy level, hence the club's interest in him, and they signed him in July 1979. At the age of 18 he was drafted into a first-team game at Brisbane Road, home of Leyton Orient. Chelsea won the game 7–3, and Pates made an impressive if hardly testing debut. Dependent upon the injury status of the first team, Pates spent much of his time

Colin Pates

in the reserves, acting as deputy to Micky Droy. By 1981, when new manager John Neal took over, he was developing quite nicely, so much so that Neal elected to build his defence around him. Although a little ungainly, he worked extremely hard under Neal's leadership and eventually took over the captain's role as his play and determination continued to grow and improve. As different managers came and went Colin Pates remained, unruffled by the backroom politics, he maintained an air of consistency and was a good captain, attempting to protect his younger players from the comings and goings at the club. Eventually, his time came out of the blue, pardon the pun, when Pates accepted a move to Charlton Athletic on loan but with a view to a permanent transfer. The Chelsea fans were in uproar, Pates was as big a part of Chelsea as anything or anyone in the 1980s, and now here he was leaving the club. The then team manager, Bobby Campbell explained that he could hardly refuse the £400,000 Charlton had offered, as he had younger more promising talent coming through and it was time to release Pates. The fans refused to accept the decision, but there was little they could do. Chelsea had lost a very good player, someone who would never be forgotten for his astute and masterful performances both on and off the field. In general, Pates was an ambassador for the club. Later he played for Brighton and Hove Albion (on loan), and Arsenal. He made 345 appearances and scored 10 goals.

PATON, JOHN. Outside-left who arrived from Glasgow Celtic after the cessation of the Second World War. Signed in November 1946 his stay at Stamford Bridge was brief, although he did manage 18 league games during the 1946/47 season, and scored 3 goals for the club. He moved back to Celtic the following season before returning to London in 1949 to play for Brentford, and later, Watford.

PAYNE, JOSEPH. England International, centre-forward Joe Payne had an illustrious career in the game. Although he was hardly a high-profile striker, he was a determined worker at each of the clubs he served. His career began at Bolsover Colliery before a move to Biggleswade Town then Luton Town in June 1934. Whilst at Kenilworth Road he grabbed an incredible 83 league goals in 72 games, a ratio which would be hard to match anywhere in the history of the game. On his league debut for the Hatters, in a match against Bristol Rovers on 13 April 1936, he scored 10 goals! Such prolific finishing could only lead to him going to a bigger club and so he arrived at Stamford Bridge in March 1938. Although he found the higher standard a little tougher than during his period at Luton, he still scored 21 league goals in 32 fixtures before the war intervened and suspended his career. After the war he moved to West Ham United in December 1946, and later joined Millwall in September 1947 before a back injury forced him to retire. A brief comeback was attempted in 1952 with Worcester City, but it was not the same Joe Payne and he eventually conceded to his injury. Joe also played first-class cricket, representing Bedfordshire in 1937.

PEACOCK, GAVIN. The career of Gavin Peacock saw him start out as a midfield player with Queen's Park Rangers, whom he joined as an apprentice, eventually signing as a full-time professional in November 1984. At Loftus Road first-team opportunities were scarce and he put in just 7 league appearances, scoring only one goal. A loan spell to Gillingham in October 1987 was turned into a permanent move in December of the same year. Some 69 league games and 11 goals later, he was off to the South coast, this time joining Bournemouth in July 1989. Having joined 3 clubs before reaching the age of 22, he could be forgiven for believing that he was going to become something of a football nomad, spending much of his career in the lower leagues. In fact, he spent just over one season at Bournemouth, making 53 league appearances and scoring 8 goals when Newcastle United stepped in to take him to St James' Park in November 1990. He was a big hit on Tyneside, as the Geordie fans recalled days of old when forwards scored goals, lots of goals. This he certainly did; 46 in 117 games and everything seemed right for him to

Gavin Peacock

remain on Tyneside for some considerable time. However, for personal reasons, nothing to do with increased wages or any sort of fall out with the club or its support, he took a move to Chelsea in August 1993 for a fee of £1.25 million. It was money well spent, as he has developed into a fine striker and utility midfielder. Always giving 100 per cent he is tireless in his running on and off the ball and never gives up until the final whistle blows.

PEARCE, IAN. Defender who was a Chelsea junior and made his way through to the fringe of the first team. He made his league debut for the Blues in the home fixture with Liverpool in May 1992 when he came on as a substitute. Incredibly, he never actually started a first-team game from when he signed in August 1991 until he was sold to Blackburn Rovers in October 1993. A real talent for the future (Rovers paid some £300,000 for his services) he scored his first league goal when he came on as a substitute in a game at Upton Park against West Ham in April 1994.

PEARSON, GEORGE. Chelsea's first ever centre-forward. A powerfully-framed individual who banged in some 18 goals in the Blues first ever season in the football league. Incredibly, he was dropped the following season, to be replaced by George Hilsdon. Any questions as to why he was dropped were quickly forgotten as his replacement soon began to rattle in the goals.

PENALTIES. In a friendly fixture with Red Banner of Hungary, in December 1954, three penalties were missed in an incredible 12-minute spell. The first was awarded to Chelsea and was duly put wide of the goal by Harris. Then Lantos missed one for Red Banner, before Harris put the third penalty straight at Olah in the Banner goal. The game finally ended in a 1–1 draw.

PHILIPS, JOHN. Tall, well-built goalkeeper who deputised for much of his Chelsea career for Peter Bonetti. Philips was a competent and most able goalkeeper, although sometimes his reflexes seemed a little slow. In a career that began with Shrewsbury Town, the Welsh International goalkeeper with 4 caps made 51 league appearances for the Gay Meadow club, before signing for Aston Villa in October 1969. He was given few chances to prove himself at Villa Park; just 15 league outings, before a move to Chelsea in August 1970. He made a total of 149 appearances for the Blues between 1970 and his release to Brighton and Hove Albion in March 1980. In between this came a spell with Crewe Alexandria. He also played for Charlton Athletic and was signed by

Crystal Palace in January 1983 but never made a league appearance for them.

PICKERING, PETER. Goalkeeper whose career began in West Yorkshire with local side Earswick. York City were the first club to notice his potential during the wartime soccer leagues, and duly signed him in April 1944. Pickering was well-built, and was strong in the air, brushing aside challenges as though they never happened. At York he made 49 league appearances before moving to Chelsea in May 1948. Opportunities for first-team football at the Bridge were limited; just 27 league games between 1948 and 1950. Non-league Kettering Town offered him a lifeline and regular first-team football. After some outstanding performances in the Kettering goal, where he needed all of his agility and dexterity to prevent some right hammerings for the Poppies, he signed for Northampton Town in July 1955 where he sent on to make 86 league appearances for the Cobblers.

PINNER, MICHAEL. Goalkeeper who played as an amateur for several clubs before turning professional with the last of his seven league clubs. Pinner was also an England amateur and was a wily character, quick to respond to shots from any angle. His career began with Pegasus before a move to Aston Villa in 1954. Three years later, after a spell with Corinthian Casuals, he joined Sheffield Wednesday. After a two-year spell at Hillsborough, he moved to Queen's Park Rangers in 1959, then to Manchester United two years later. He joined Chelsea as an amateur in October 1961 and made just one appearance for the club before signing for Swansea City seven months later. He finally turned professional in October 1962 when he signed for Leyton Orient. Few players have played for so many top clubs, yet achieved so little.

PLUM, SETH. Tiny wing-half who gained International recognition for his country, England, in 1923 whilst with Charlton Athletic. His playing days began with Tottenham Park, Avondale, before a move to Barnet, then on to

Charlton Athletic in 1922. He was good at breaking down the opposition attack and reading the game, it was his distribution which was suspect. He arrived at Chelsea in March 1924 and was an industrious little figure, always working hard in the defence. His passing did improve as he matured and gained more composure on the ball. He moved to Southend United in 1927.

POINTS—MOST. The most number of points the club have ever accumulated was in the 1988/89 season when they amassed a massive 99 points to win the 2nd division championship.

PORTERFIELD, IAN. Team manager June 1981 to February 1993. As a player Ian Porterfield had a fairly undistinguished time, his greatest moment arriving in May 1973 when he scored the winning goal in the shock FA Cup final victory over Leeds United. He began his managerial career with Rotherham United in 1979 before taking over at Sheffield United in June 1981. He won promotion from the respective leagues for both clubs. Having won the 4th division Championship with Sheffield United, they were promoted the next season. Incredibly, he was sacked by the club when results began to turn. He then took over at Aberdeen when Alex Ferguson moved to Manchester United in 1986. Having left Scotland in May 1988, he took up the assistant manager's role at Chelsea in November 1989 but left after a few days to take over as manager of Reading, where he remained until 1991.

Porterfield left Elm Park to take up the manager's job at the Bridge in June 1991. An honest man, he knew he had a lot of hard work ahead of him, however there was a good deal of quality within the squad with the likes of Tony Dorigo, and Gordon Durie. To the absolute amazement of all Chelsea fans, he proceeded to dismantle this squad, selling Dorigo to Leeds and Durie to Tottenham Hotspur. Neither player was replaced with anyone of similar quality. Youngsters were brought in, and although their ability was not in question, they lacked the experience and professionalism of those now departed. Porterfield had all the right motives and reasons for rebuilding the team, but perhaps it was all a little too sudden. He undoubtedly underestimated some players' ability and over-rated his own instincts to replace these with younger, fresher talent. He was full of self-belief which in the end wasn't enough to take the club to higher plains. He was sacked in February 1993 when his Chelsea team had gone a horrendous two months without a win. Porterfield was allegedly surprised at being shown the door, perhaps indicative of his self-opinion. Despite this he was enthusiastic about his role and always made time to acknowledge fans.

PRIESTLEY, JOHN. Half-back who arrived from Irish club side Coleraine in 1925. A Northern Ireland International, he was a solid player if perhaps a little eccentric. He wore a skull cap whilst playing (see *Curiosity*), this aroused more than its fair share of banter from the terracing, but never seemed to affect his game. In 1934 he was forced to give up the game in England and so returned to his native Ireland. Always one to be different, his career-wrecking injury was received as a result of some mud getting into his eye!

PROGRAMME. Over the years, Chelsea's programme has taken on many different guises. It was originally titled *The Chelsea FC Chronicle* before taking on the more archetypal format of football programmes as we now know them. Chelsea programmes have always been collectable with many rare issues bringing in astronomical prices. Obviously the early issues are the most valuable, however those from the Championship season of 1955 are also much sought after items.

PROMOTION. Chelsea FC have been promoted on no less than 7 occasions, always from the 2nd division to the 1st. These promotions took place in: 1906/07, 1911/12, 1929/30, 1962/63, 1976/77, all as runners up, 1983/84, 1988/89 as Champions.

PROUDFOOT, PETER. Workman-like defender-cum-half-back, he was rugged and unafraid of any dangers in the tackle or awkward challenge. He gave it out and expected to take it back. Peter Proudfoot's career began with Scottish club side St Mirren before a move to Lincoln City in 1900. Four years later, in October 1904, he arrived in London with Millwall, and a short time later moved to Clapton Orient. He signed for Chelsea in April 1906 but found himself in and out of the first team, more out than in. He remained with the Blues for a very short period, his attitude was that if he couldn't get into the first team, then he should move on. So he went on to trials with Manchester United reserves before transferring to Stockport County in 1908. After retiring from the playing side of the game, he managed Clapton Orient on three separate occasions.

Q

QUALITY PERFORMANCES. Everyone has their own personal favourites in this category, for example, the 2–0 victory over FC Bruges in the 1994/95 UEFA Cup in March 1995, when, 1–0 down from the first leg, the Blues put in a very professional performance in the second leg at the Bridge to win through 2–1 on aggregate.

Another potential candidate is the 7–1 thrashing of Leeds United in a 1st division fixture on 16 March 1935, in which striker Joe Bambrick put 4 in the net. Chelsea overpowered their Yorkshire rivals in all departments. In what was a topsy-turvy season, the Blues were themselves on the wrong side of a hiding just one month later, when Wolverhampton Wanderers slammed 6 past them at Molineux.

Perhaps the most notable performance by any Chelsea team has to be the European Cup Winners Cup victory over Jeunesse Hautcharage at Stamford Bridge which was comfortably won 13–0. Every Chelsea fan at that particular game will recall the crowd's cheers as the part-timers from Luxembourg were taught a cruel European lesson. Had it not been for some brave goalkeeping the margin might have been even greater. Few performances have warranted so much praise so this result has to take pride of place in this category.

If pushed, I would have to say that the final of the 1970/71 European Cup Winners Cup in which the Blues faced, and beat, a strong Real Madrid side 3–2 on aggregate has to be a close second. This was the night when Chelsea proved their true quality and European status.

QUICKEST GOAL. Another controversial category; it has recently been claimed that Chris Sutton's goal for Blackburn at Everton was the quickest to be scored in the Premier League. However, John Spencer netted a goal against Leicester City in October 1994 which cannot have been far outside this time. Virtually straight from the kick off, a ball was crossed from the right and Spencer launched himself at the ball heading it sweetly into the back of the net in front of the temporary South stand. This arguably is the quickest goal the Blues have scored in a competitive fixture.

R

RANDALL, ERNEST. Inside-forward signed from Bognor Regis Town in December 1950. The transition from non-league to league football still remains a great one. So it takes a player of some quality to leap in at the deep end and be able to pick up his game. Ernie Randall struggled even though he did have a nice touch when cutting infield from wide positions. It was his pace, however, which had initially attracted Chelsea. He made 3 league appearances and scored one goal before he was transferred to Crystal Palace in June 1953. He eventually slipped back into the relative obscurity of the non-league game.

RECORD. Chelsea released the almost legendary *Blue is the Colour* record on 45rpm in 1972. It actually reached number 5 in the pop charts of the era. Twenty-three years later and it is still on sale in the club shop, although now it is recorded on compact disc. The record has outlasted any by the most popular music groups, so take that!

REID, ERNEST. A right full-back who arrived via Swansea City in September 1937. Reid had been spotted playing for his local club side Troedyrhiw in July 1932 when the Swans signed him. He was a stocky, powerful defender, tough in the tackle and very strong in all areas of his game. Perhaps because of his lack of finesse he made just one league appearance in 1938 when the outbreak of the Second World War disrupted his career.

In June 1945, when hostilities had ceased, he signed for Norwich City, but again he struggled to make any impact at Carrow Road, making just 5 league appearances for the Canaries.

REPLAYS. The most famous of all replays in which Chelsea have featured is the FA Cup final victory over Leeds United in 1970. However, in the 1955/56 competition the club drew Burnley in the fourth round. The first game at Turf Moor ended in a 1–1 draw, then the replay at Stamford Bridge four days later also ended in a 1–1 draw, this after extra time. Five days later, on 6 February 1956 the clubs met again, this time at St Andrews, home of Birmingham City, and this time they played out a 2–2 draw, again with extra time. A third replay then took place at Highbury, Arsenal's ground on 13 February 1956; again, with extra time being played, the result was 0–0. Finally a fourth replay was scheduled, eventually taking place at White Hart Lane, Tottenham, on 15 February, and this time Chelsea won through 2–0 with goals from Tindall and Lewis. After all that trouble to get through, Chelsea were knocked out of the competition three days later by Everton 1–0!

RHOADES-BROWN, PETER. Signed as an apprentice in July 1979, Peter Rhoades-Brown was a rather classy player who operated on the left wing. His lean frame was nimble rather than strong and he would drop his shoulder and send defenders the wrong way then nip in and out of others thus avoiding the occasional lunging challenge. At times, when the going got tough, Rhoades-Brown would disappear; this was not his kind of game, he was a footballer rather than a ball winner. He made a total of 97 appearances for the club between 1979 and 1983, scoring just 5 goals; a poor average for a winger, but indicative of his attitude to getting in where it hurts. He moved to Oxford United in January 1984 where he became a first-team regular and still, after his retirement from playing, works for the club, as a football in the community official.

ROBERTS, GRAHAM. Born in Southampton, Graham Roberts first signed for the Saints' closest rivals, Portsmouth, from Sholing in March 1977. His time at Fratton Park was one of development, as he never made a league appearance for Pompey, and was at the time on non-contract terms. He returned to the non-league scene with Weymouth when Pompey refused to make any firm

Graham Roberts

offer for his skills, a decision which they must greatly regret to this day. At Weymouth he was a goliath, winning 'man of the match' awards on a regular basis. Tottenham Hotspur then stepped in to take him to White Hart Lane where he became one of the most cultured central defenders in the first division. Strong, and tough in the tackle, he was a real motivator as his battling performances often kick-started others into pulling all the stops out. England honours followed, 6 full caps, as his stature and game improved. A big money move to Glasgow Rangers, where he became something of a cult figure took place in 1986. Roberts knew the game inside out and his experience was a major factor in the 'Gers' success during his two-year spell at Ibrox. Indeed, there was an outcry when Rangers allowed him to leave in August 1988. Fans attempted to influence the club to keep him, some supporters even tried to raise funds to pay his wages just to keep him in Glasgow and Graham Roberts fan clubs existed all over Scotland. There was mayhem, but Rangers had taken a brave decision. It was at this time that he arrived at Chelsea and took on the mantle of the captain's role. His leadership skills and reading of the game were a revelation in the heart of the Chelsea defence, but these were not his only talents, for he weighed in with some 22 goals in 83 matches. He was eventually sold to West Bromwich Albion with his playing days now in their twilight stage. Roberts earned the respect of every supporter of every club he played for. He may have had a strong, nasty image on the pitch, but off it he was a real ambassador, attending supporters' functions, not because he had to, but because he wanted to!

ROBERTS, JOHN. Australian-born goalkeeper who came to England for trials and was signed by Chelsea in January 1966. His previous club had been Leichardt (Aus). A tall man, he never received the opportunity of furthering his career at Stamford Bridge, for within three months of signing him, he was transferred to Blackburn Rovers. He later played for Chesterfield, Bradford City, Southend United and Northampton Town.

ROBERTSON, JOHN-TAIT. Team manager April 1905 – October 1906. A left-half, he first played for Morton in 1896 before moving into the English game in 1898 with Everton, then Southampton. He returned to Scotland in 1899 when Glasgow Rangers paid £300 for his services, but it was back to England, and London in April when he took on the role as Chelsea player/manager when the club was looking to make a name for itself in the football league. Having served at so many clubs he had made an incredible number of contacts which he used to his and Chelsea's benefit. The club's first season in the league was a reasonably successful one, as they finished third in the 2nd division, with some memorable results; the thrashings of Barnsley and Blackpool, 6–0, Hull City, 5–1, Orient, 6–1, and Port Vale, 7–0. However, in the FA Cup, they were ignominiously dumped out in the third qualifying round, 7–1 by Crystal Palace. It was a good start to the club's league career, and Jackie Robertson was a good manager for the club. He played on 39 occasions during that first season and laid the foundations for the future of Chelsea FC.

He moved on from Chelsea to take over as player/manager of Glossop in October 1906 where he remained until 1909 when he took up a coaching role on the continent. He returned to the English game in 1927 as trainer/coach with Coventry City. The man who took Chelsea into their first ever league campaign died on 24 January 1935 at the relatively young age of 58.

ROBERTSON, WILLIAM. G. Billy Robertson was signed from Scottish non-league side Arthurlie in July 1946. He was a goalkeeper who persevered and made a great name for himself at Stamford Bridge. Stocky, yet elegant and perceptive, he was the master of his own penalty area. He had no speciality, and although it is difficult to comprehend, he was a good all-round goalkeeper who worked at at improving his skills, believing that there was always room for improvement. His performances provided some stability in the defence as Chelsea went on to win the 1st Division Championship. He made a total of 214 appearances for Chelsea between July 1946 and September 1960 when he transferred to Leyton Orient. A marvellous club servant and a credit to the Championship side of 1955, he sadly passed away in 1973.

ROBERTSON, WILLIAM. H. Goalkeeper signed from RAF Lossiemouth in September 1945 and, coincidentally, first-team keeper until Bill Robertson (the second) arrived in 1946. Bill Robertson was not to have a distinguished career at Chelsea, mainly because of the competition for places after the war. He was a reflex keeper and a good shot-stopper, but he lacked that assertiveness one likes to see in a goalkeeper. He made 37 league appearances for Chelsea between October 1945 and December 1948 when he was transferred to Birmingham City. He later had a distinguished career with Stoke City.

ROBEY, GEORGE. A popular music hall comedian of the early part of the 20th Century. Robey's act included some odd routines which were perhaps better suited to the circus than a music hall, as he jumped, danced, and denigrated himself to the amusement of his audience. Incredibly in 1905, Robey was signed by Chelsea as an amateur. Whether this was an early form of publicity stunt or whether Robey was actually a footballer of reasonable quality is open to debate. However, his signing ensures that Chelsea were given a great deal of publicity in the music halls and media of the day who treated his signing as something of a joke. A favourite, if not over used statement by music hall comedians was, 'Is there anyone from Chelsea FC in here tonight? No, that's good at least I don't have to worry about my body swerve.' Hardly amusing, but enough to raise a laugh in the Edwardian era.

ROBSON, ROBERT. Ex-manager of England national side and various English and European club sides. Bobby was actually a scout for Chelsea in 1968 before taking on the Ipswich Town manager's job in January 1969.

ROBSON, BRYAN (POP). No matter what others may say, there really is only one 'Pop' Robson, others are merely pretenders to his title. Pop was a prolific goalscorer and a player who could read the game as well as any forward I have seen. His career began with Newcastle United in November 1962 where he made well over 200 appearances for the Magpies before being sold to West Ham United in 1971. His goals for the Hammers always seemed to be spectacular efforts, scissor kicks or arrogant lobs and volleys. Three years later he joined his home town club, Sunderland but things didn't go as planned; the team were struggling to live up to their outstanding FA Cup success of the previous season and it was hoped Pop would be the catalyst for more success, and although he netted some 34 league goals he was not settled. He moved back to West Ham United in 1976 before returning to Sunderland in 1979.

Then came a move to Brunton Park, Carlisle in 1981 where he enjoyed success as the club won promotion to the 2nd Division with Pop among their leading scorers, in fact so good was his play that Chelsea signed him in August 1982. This was a move which upset many Carlisle supporters. In reality it was a short-term affair, as he made just 12 appearances for the Blues scoring 5 goals. He then returned to Carlisle on loan. Just as the Cumbrians were about to sign him, Sunderland whisked him away from under their noses. He spent one season at Roker Park before coming back to Carlisle for the final time in July 1984. With his playing days all but finished, he made just 10 further league appearances before taking over as manager, but resigned shortly after. He had a spell back in the North East before taking on a coaching role at Old Trafford. With 2 England U23 caps under his belt and representation at Football League level it remains something of a mystery as to why he never got an England full International call up!

ROBSON, THOMAS. Winger who was signed from Northampton Town in December 1965, Tommy Robson was tricky, articulate and above all intelligent with the ball at his feet. He remained at Chelsea for two half-seasons, playing in the remainder of the '65/66 and beginning of the '66/67. His form was erratic and this kept him out of the limelight for long periods at a time, just 6 appearances were made before he was sold to Newcastle United in December 1966. He later joined Peterborough United where he became a regular first-teamer for almost 12 years.

ROCASTLE, DAVID. Born in Lewisham, David Rocastle first signed for Arsenal in December 1984 and proved to be a marvellous talent. A midfielder, he possessed all the skills one would expect from the archetypal South American-style footballer. Cool, calm and calculating, Rocastle progressed to be one of the finest midfielders in the country whilst at Highbury. A shock move to Leeds United in July 1992 saw the Gunners receive £2 million for his services as Rocky moved to the League Champions. After a marvellous pre-season at Elland Road, in which he showed why Leeds paid so much for his services, Rocky was, incredibly, dropped from first-team football. Nobody knew why Leeds boss Howard Wilkinson refused to play him, when he did get into the side, he was awesome, with the Yorkshire club's fans rejoicing in his glory and singing his name constantly. Despite this, the Leed's boss refused to accept that he was first-team material at Elland Road, and the tone was set for what has to be the worst two seasons of his career. In December 1993, he was swapped to Manchester City in a player exchange for David White, a player of the same ilk who some claim has considerably less talent than Rocky! Rocky's move to Maine Road saw some consistency return to his game as his name became one of the first on the team sheet.

Within a short space of time he was again showing the qualities which had made him such an outstanding player prior to his move to Leeds. In 1994 he moved to Chelsea in a £1.2 million transfer, with City desperately requiring the money to rebuild rather than there being anything wrong with Rocky's play. Since his move back to London he has settled down nicely into the way of things at Chelsea, but seems to have lost a little of his old confidence which can at times affect his play.

Rocky is a player who has the ability to rise to the occasion and will, I am certain, prove well worth the money

Glenn Hoddle has invested in him. A playmaker, he can on his good days completely control a game. He is an accomplished England International.

ROFE, DENNIS. A thick-set and strong full-back whose career has been perhaps more spectacular elsewhere, although he was a big hit with the Chelsea support who saw him as the new McCreadie or Chopper Harris. His game was all about getting the ball at all costs and preventing the opposition from scoring, if he could not get the ball then sadly it had to be the man. His style was controversial, but he was hugely effective.

He joined Leyton Orient in February 1968 then moved to Leicester City in 1972. At Filbert Street he became a consistent performer making somewhere in the region of 300 appearances. He joined Chelsea, his third club, in February 1980 and was to make 60 appearances in the blue shirt before a move to Southampton in July 1982. Despite his rough attitude to the game, he was, in his later years, something of a perfectionist as his passing and experience allowed him to do more than just punt it clear. If only as a youngster he could have shown such quality, then he may well have won more honours.

ROUGVIE, DOUGLAS. Another hard man, Doug Rougvie joined Chelsea from Aberdeen in August 1984 and immediately made a first-team place his own, commandeering a role in the defence. The spirit of his play was understandably solid, he took no nonsense from clever, tricky wingers, and once he had won the ball, it was up to him to put it out of danger and hopefully to another Chelsea player. His weakness was in his passing, especially the long ball which could literally end up anywhere. However, as a defender, he was very good at what he did especially in aerial combat when he would not only win the ball, but direct it nine times out of ten to another Chelsea player; his head was far more accurate than his feet. In 100 performances he scored 3 goals before a move to Brighton and Hove Albion in June 1987. Later he played for Shrewsbury Town and Fulham.

Doug Rougvie

ROUSE, FREDERICK. An inside-forward who signed for Chelsea in 1907. He was the club's first ever four-figure transfer, with a fee of £1,000 going to his previous club, Stoke City. Rouse was a robust player who harried and hassled defenders. Tricky when on the ball, he had the uncanny ability of running flat out before suddenly stopping dead and unleashing a terrific shot, all in one movement. Few defenders of his era could hold him, such was his tenacity.

S

SAUNDERS, DEREK. Wing-half who signed from local non-league side, Walthamstow Avenue, Saunders turned professional in July 1953. An influential player who was the backbone of a defence which conceded just 57 goals during the 1955 Championship campaign. A busy player, he was a ball winner and a tenacious character who appeared for England amateurs and was unfortunate never to break into the full International scene. He was a one-club man and remained at Stamford Bridge between 1953 and 1958 making 203 league appearances with 9 goals.

SAUNDERS, JOHN. Central defender who arrived via Darlington where he made 67 league appearances shortly after the Second World War. He joined Chelsea in May 1948 and remained with the club for six years making 52 league appearances. He became something of a squad player, mainly through injuries and inconsistent play. It had been hoped that he would progress into one of the finest centre-halfs in the country, however, it never materialised, as he was, at times, slow to react and seemingly unsure of himself. He went on to play for Crystal Palace who signed him in August 1954, and then later for Chester City.

SCORERS. The Blues' record scorer in any one league season is Jimmy Greaves, with 41 goals in the 1960/61 season. The club's record goalscorer of all time is Bobby Tambling, with 164 goals, between 1958 and 1970.

SCORERS—ODDITY. In the 1962/63 season, Bobby Tambling scored 12 goals in 13 games. Incredibly, he then encountered a barren spell where he never scored for three months! He finished the season as the club's top scorer with 23 goals! Peter Osgood scored in every round of the 1969/70 season's FA Cup tournament; one against Birmingham in the third round, one against Burnley in the fourth round, one against Crystal Palace in the fifth round, 3 against Queen's Park Rangers in the sixth round, and one against Watford in the semi-final. He rounded the season off with an equalising goal against Leeds in the Final replay at Old Trafford.

SCOTT, MELVYN. Signed from the juniors and turned professional in November 1956, Mel Scott was an effervescent character and a fine centre-half. His constant chat to fellow defenders during the game ensured that the defence worked in unison. An England U23 International and England Youth International, he was a player who could perform with the best. He remained with the club until March 1963 when he joined Brentford. He made 97 league appearances for the Blues without scoring!

SEXTON, DAVID. Team manager October 1967 – October 1974. The son of British middleweight boxer Archie Sexton, a challenger for the British title in 1933, Dave was born in Islington, North London and began his playing career with Newmarket Town, before moves to Chelmsford City, Luton Town, West Ham United, Leyton Orient, Brighton and Hove Albion, and Crystal Palace, with whom he retired as a player in the 1961/62 season. His last competitive game was at Workington's Borough Park on 25 February 1960, in a 1–1 draw. February 1962 saw him move to Stamford Bridge as assistant coach to Tommy Docherty, before a move into management with Leyton Orient in January 1965. This was an unsuccessful partnership and he resigned 11 months later, with the O's at the bottom of the league. There then followed a spell as coach at Fulham before he took on the role of Arsenal coach and assistant manager.

In October 1967 he returned to the Bridge as team manager replacing his old boss, Tommy Docherty, a situation which would be repeated later in both men's careers. After taking the Blues to FA Cup and European Cup Winners Cup successes in 1970 and 1971 respectively, Sexton found the pressure slowly building around him. The club built an impressive three-tier (East) stand which virtually bankrupted them, the result being that no money was available for new signings. The pressure was further exacerbated when Sexton had disagreements with several of his first-team stars, resulting in their departure from the club. This created incoming finances and allowed for the occasional dabble on the transfer market. Before he knew it, Sexton had destroyed the very heart of his successful side. Try as he may he never won over the fans, and it came as no real surprise when he was ignominiously sacked in October 1974. A quietly-spoken and shy man, he handled the dismissal with great dignity. He was not out of work long, 13 days to be precise before taking the helm at Queen's Park Rangers. However, he left there to take over the hot seat at Manchester United, again replacing Tommy Docherty, whose personal life had become involved with his professional circumstances. Sexton later managed Coventry City and has been assistant manager of the England national side. He is currently coach to the England U21 team and is still one of the most respected men in the game.

SHAW, COLIN. As a youngster, Colin Shaw was impressive in the Hertfordshire leagues. An inside-forward, he had a good strike rate at junior level, sufficient to warrant Chelsea taking a gamble on his services and signing him as a professional in May 1960, after he had spent some time playing for the youth side. He made a solitary appearance in 1961 before a move to Norwich City in August 1963. He later played for Leyton Orient.

SHEARER, DUNCAN. Today, Shearer is one of the most prolific scorers in the game. It seems that he has matured with age, and now possesses a certain coolness, sometimes mistaken for arrogance in front of goal. He signed for Chelsea from Inverness Clach, in November 1983, and made just 2 appearances for the club, scoring one goal before a move to Huddersfield Town in March 1986. At Leeds Road he was a big success, honing his goal-scoring abilities. He later transferred to Swindon Town then to Blackburn Rovers, followed by a move to Scotland with Aberdeen. A fine goal taker, what he lacks on the skill front is more than made up by a hunger to put the ball in the back of the net. One of the most underrated strikers of his time.

SHELLITO, KENNETH. Dependable right-back, Ken Shellito was a product of the junior set up, having been scouted as a schoolboy playing for Sutton School, Hornchurch. He signed professional for Chelsea in April 1957 and went on to make 123 appearances for the club, grabbing 2 goals into the bargain. An England International, he earned his solitary cap in a game against Czechoslovakia in 1963. He was forced to retire from playing in January 1969 but took up a position as youth team coach. As a player he was remarkably quick for such a thick-set full-back. His educated right foot meant he could trap the ball, pass it and strike it as well as any forward. At times his brave play would let him down when he would get caught out of position advancing up the field.

In July 1977 he was promoted to first-team manager, but had very little success during his tenure. Indeed, when he left, in December 1978, the club were bottom of the 1st division and heading back to the 2nd division. It was a sad end to a fine Chelsea career. He later enjoyed spells in management with Queen's Park Rangers, Crystal Palace, Preston North End and Cambridge United, as well as a brief spell as coach at Wolverhampton Wanderers.

SHERWOOD, STEPHEN. An apprentice who broke through to the first team in 1971 having turned professional in July of that year. He had been impressive in reserve fixtures and seemed surprisingly confident for such a slim-line individual.

Steve was given the opportunity to play league football only when injuries forced other keepers to stand down. He made 17 appearances in the Chelsea goal before being sold to Watford in November 1976. He also had loan spells with Millwall and Brentford. Later he played for Grimsby Town and Northampton Town. A nervous goalkeeper, he lacked the confidence to see him through a full 90 minutes; one moment he would be brilliant, the next dreadful. His one weakness was the crossed ball, which was never more obvious than in the FA Cup final of 1984 when he failed to hold a simple cross under a challenge from Everton striker, Andy Gray. Some claimed it to be an unfair challenge, but those who had watched Sherwood's game knew different. This is a great shame, as he is good professional who has served the game well. Some keepers seem to prefer to remain anonymous, Steve Sherwood was one such individual.

SHIPPERLEY, NEIL. Striker born in Chatham, Kent. Neil Shipperley was a bright young prospect making his Premier league debut at Southampton in 1993 at the age of 19. Although not the tallest of strikers he does have a good touch, which can take him neatly round defenders. His goal at Elland Road, Leeds, in the 1993/4 season was taken with all the finesse of a player with far greater experience, running onto the ball and lifting it over an advancing keeper from a tight angle. In 1994 he moved to Southampton, where team manager Alan Ball is nurturing him and providing him with all the experience he will need to become a great striker. Such opportunities were limited at Stamford Bridge due to the quantity of quality players available. Shipperley has recently gained honours as an England U21 International. Whether he will progress to full International level is very much down to his commitment and willingness to learn.

SILLETT, JOHN. Signed from Southampton in 1954 where he was an amateur, John Sillett followed his brother, Peter to Stamford Bridge. Tall and stocky he was a difficult man to beat, as he stood up to attackers and made important lunging tackles time and again to disarm the attack.

He made a career total of 102 appearances for Chelsea, scoring one goal. He was sold to Coventry City in April 1962 and later played for Plymouth Argyle. As a manager he took Coventry City to success in the FA Cup but could not maintain the winning formula in the league. He is one of the game's real characters, a nice man to meet and a great man to listen to.

SILLETT, PETER. Although his brother would not appreciate me saying this, Peter was the better of the two players. A full-back, he signed for Southampton in June 1950 and made some 59 league appearances for the Saints, scoring 4 goals. He joined Chelsea in June 1953 and was part of the 1955 Championship-winning team. He will be remembered by many Chelsea fans for his huge kicking ability, literally launching the ball from defence deep into the opposition's half. He was, however, a one-footed player; his left foot hardly ever kicked the ball. An England full International, he made 3 appearances for his country against France, Spain and Portugal in 1955, all whilst playing for Chelsea. He also won International honours at England Youth, U23, and 'B' team level. He made some 284 appearances and scored 34 goals before a move out of the professional game and into management with Ashford.

SIMNER, JOSEPH. First appeared for Folkestone Town shortly after the end of the Second World War. He came to Chelsea in October 1947 as an attacker with a big reputation in the Kent leagues. However, reputations in football count for nothing, Simner was never able to prove his worth and was given just one first-team run out in 1947. Having failed to deliver the goods, he spent the rest of his Chelsea career in the reserves. He moved to Swindon Town in July 1949.

SINCLAIR, FRANK. A defender and a very capable one at that. Frankie is one of the Chelsea favourites, his fiery determination to do well occasionally rubs off onto his team-mates inspiring them on to better performances. He has few bad games, many average ones, but still gives a whole-hearted effort. He was signed through the Youth Team in May 1990 and has since improved and matured into a fine player. A loan spell with West Bromwich Albion in December 1991 was there for him to profit from and he gave a good account of himself at the Hawthorns but never envisaged a move away from Chelsea. Indeed the club are unlikely to sell one of their prize possessions, as anyone who watches Chelsea will know, he is a star.

SINCLAIR, WILLIAM. Wing-half from Scottish club side Morton, Sinclair signed in September 1964 and made just one appearance during the 1964/65 season. A player who seemed lost in the English game, he remained at the club for just one season.

SISSONS, JOHN. A player who had a distinguished career elsewhere and arrived at Stamford Bridge as very much his last port of call. Chelsea felt that his presence in the dressing room would influence the younger element within the team. John Sissons was an England Schools, Youth and U23 International. He played first for West Ham United where he won many honours and made over 200 appearances on the left wing. In 1970, he joined Sheffield Wednesday before moving to East Anglia with Norwich City in 1973. He never seemed settled outside London and so returned to join Chelsea in August 1974, making his first-team debut against Carlisle United on the opening day of the season. He struggled with fitness and, after making 9 consecutive starts at the beginning of the season, he made just one more all season. His career total for Chelsea was just 10 games.

SMART, JAMES. Another young player who failed to make it in the English game. Jimmy Smart had been monitored whilst playing for Morton in Scotland. A winger, he possessed the speed and ball control which it was hoped would carry him onto greater things. He was brought to

Chelsea in February 1965, and made one appearance. To be fair, the side at this time was filled with players who were to become established stars, so it was always going to be difficult for a youngster to break through.

SMETHURST, DEREK. South African-born striker, Derek Smethurst was signed from Durban City in December 1968. He made his first-team debut on 1 September 1970 in a 0–0 draw with Burnley at Turf Moor. His first Chelsea goal came in the 4–1 rout of West Bromwich Albion at Stamford Bridge in January 1971. A strong, bustling inside-forward, he fed off Osgood but was somewhat inconsistent for the full 90 minutes. He made 18 appearances and scored 5 goals and was sold to Millwall in September 1971 where he became a first-team regular.

SMITH, JAMES. Jimmy Smith was a dour Yorkshireman but a terrific footballer. Born in Sheffield, he moved to London with Chelsea in April 1951 having previously played for Shildon. His sense of positioning was outstanding, as he ran onto through balls and pulled them back or laid them off for his colleagues with unerring consistency and accuracy. Although a very good crosser of the dead ball, a ball on the move presented him with other problems. He made 19 league appearances and scored 3 goals between 1953 and a move to Leyton Orient in July 1955.

SMITH, ROBERT. Giant of a centre-forward and full England International who made 15 appearances for his country between 1961–1964. Bobby Smith began playing football at Lingdale School before moving to Redcar Boys Club, Redcar United, and Chelsea in 1949, before signing professional in May 1950. Very much a novice, he learned his trade at Stamford Bridge, making 74 league appearances and banging in 23 goals. He moved to Tottenham Hotspur in December 1955 and progressed to greater things. He became Spurs' regular centre-forward in a 9-year spell at White Hart Lane, finishing moves created and crafted by other, more talented, individuals. Later played for Brighton and having retired from the game after a spell with Hastings

United, became a van driver! Can you imagine today's stars (as Bobby Smith very much was in the early 1960s) doing the same? I sincerely doubt it!

SPACKMAN, NIGEL. Dependable midfielder, tall and athletic with an appetite for control of the ball. Spackman was a tireless workhorse when he came to Chelsea via Bournemouth in June 1983. A good all-round player, he spent three seasons in the Chelsea midfield and was quality personified as countless soccer pundits cooed over his marvellous passing ability, or his finishing in front of goal, even his heading power was above average.

He was, during his time with Chelsea, categorised as one of the best midfielders in the country which is why Liverpool bought him in February 1987. At Anfield he became a little injury prone so his appearances were limited. A move to Queen's Park Rangers in February 1989 gave him the opportunity to rebuild his career in first-team football. So impressive was he that Glasgow Rangers, then the top buying club in Britain, took him to Ibrox Stadium in November 1989 for a fee of around £500,000. In August 1992 he returned to Chelsea for a fee of £485,000 proving just how valuable he was to his respective clubs. Spackman is still cool, calm and collected on the ball. Although his pace has receded just a little, he is still one of the best distributors of the ball in the side. Neither his appetite for the game, nor his tenacity on the pitch have diminished and he continues to urge his teammates on to fight, fight, fight for Chelsea.

SPARROW, JOHN. Left-back who won honours as an England Schoolboy and was in the England Youth side. He signed professional from the youth team in August 1974. An underestimated player in the Chelsea line-up, he was never over-rawed by the situation, and gave total commitment in every game. He made 68 first-team outings between August 1974 and January 1981 when he joined Exeter City. In between he enjoyed a short loan spell at Millwall. He made his Chelsea debut at Leicester City in 1975, scoring his first goal in a 2–1 reversal to Middlesbrough later that same season.

161

SPECTOR, MILES. A junior who progressed through to the first team in 1953, and made 3 league appearances on the left wing during the 1952/53 season. He remained an amateur and moved to Millwall, after a spell with Hendon, still on amateur forms, in May 1956.

SPEEDIE, DAVID. Scotland International David Speedie is the kind of player who either endears himself to fans or creates animosity, such is his skill and character. Most opposition fans tend to dislike him, believing him arrogant and a physical, dirty-style player. Granted, there is an element of professionalism to his game, as he can make ankle taps seem as though they are leg breakers, but what footballer doesn't? Speedie, the footballer, is quick, smooth and mercenary which is why he has played for so many of the top clubs in the land. His career began with Barnsley in 1978, then came a move to Darlington in 1980. Chelsea signed him in June 1982 and it was at Stamford Bridge where he made his name. A neat, almost diminutive player, he forged a good professional relationship with Kerry Dixon. The pair were a formidable partnership, with each seemingly providing goals for the other.

Speedie was most at home when running onto the ball or taking it in the penalty area, he could turn and shoot on a sixpence. He made 197 appearances for the Blues, scoring 64 goals, before he moved to Coventry City in 1987. He later played for Liverpool and Blackburn Rovers, and is currently on Leicester City's books. A tenacious character he was never one to admit defeat, fighting for the ball right up to the final whistle, and sometimes after!

SPENCE, RICHARD. Outside-right whose career began at his home town club of Barnsley in South Yorkshire. Spence was a small player who could turn his man inside out. Defenders would occasionally let fly at him, only to find that he had jinked to the left, or the right and was away, leaving them looking rather foolish. Signed from Thorpe Colliery in February 1933 he made 64 league appearances

David Speedie

for the Tykes before signing for Chelsea in October 1934. He was an instant success at Stamford Bridge, where he employed his trickery as much as possible and seemed to relish the bigger audiences Chelsea attracted. An England International he played for his country against Austria and Belgium in 1936. He made some 280 plus appearances for Chelsea between 1934 and 1947, though his career was interrupted by the hostilities of the Second World War. When he retired from playing, he remained at the club as a member of the training staff.

SPENCER, JOHN. Striker from Glasgow Rangers who signed for the Blues in August 1992 for a fee of £450,000, and has since proved a real bargain buy. Although somewhat small for a striker, John has a big heart, loads of commitment, and stacks of goals behind him to prove his worth. He made his Chelsea debut against Norwich in August 1992 and scored his first Chelsea goal at home to Manchester City in January 1993. One of his finest strikes came in the 1993/94 season, a sweet, dropping volley against Leeds United at Stamford Bridge, struck from 20

John Spencer

yards. Indeed, he seems to like scoring against the Yorkshire club, netting twice in a 3–2 victory at Elland Road in the early weeks of the 94/95 season. He has recently been called up into the Scotland full International squad, and may well prove difficult to oust once he establishes himself.

STANLEY, GARRY. Began his career with Chelsea signing professional forms in March 1971, but not making his first-team debut until 1975. Garry Stanley was a neat, midfield player, never afraid of getting stuck in. He made some 115 appearances, netting 15 goals between 1971 and August 1978 when he joined Everton. He also played for Swansea City, and was outstanding during their first division days. He went on to play for Portsmouth, Witchita USA and Bristol City.

STEFFEN, WILLIAM. Swiss International defender, Bill Steffen was signed after the Second World War, in November 1946. He made 15 appearances in 1946 as an amateur.

STEIN, MARK. Before Mark Stein arrived at Chelsea he had, so to speak, travelled the circuit. He initially signed for Luton Town in January 1984, then moved to Aldershot on loan in January 1986 before a £300,000 transfer to Queen's Park Rangers in August 1988. Just over a year later he was on his way to Oxford United, in a player exchange deal.

It was Stoke City who kick-started his career when they snapped him up for a fee of £100,000 in September 1991. Chelsea payed £1.5 million for him in October 1993. Although not a tall player for a striker, he climbs well and can be a match for the biggest central defender. Stein is at home on the ground, facing the goal, juggling with the ball and attacking defenders before letting loose a ferocious shot. He is an adaptable goalscorer, playing in any of the front positions and able to shoot with his left or right foot. His goals have been a revelation for the Blues, particularly when he links up with John Spencer to form a formidable partnership.

STEPNEY, ALEXANDER. England International goalkeeper who made his sole appearance in 1968 against

165

Mark Stein

Sweden in a 3–1 victory which was only slightly soured by his conceding of a goal on his debut.

He began his career as a player with Tooting and Mitcham signing for Millwall in May 1963. He was a lean and agile keeper, who made some excellent reflex saves. He signed for Chelsea in May 1966, making one appearance before being sold to Manchester United in September of the same year. He has the dubious honour of having been beaten by another goalkeeper, when Pat Jennings scored from his own penalty area against him, lofting the ball high in the air, and bouncing it straight over Stepney's head.

STRIDE, DAVID. Apprentice who signed professional terms in January 1976. He made his league debut against Birmingham City in September 1978 and went on to make 37 appearances as left-back. He moved to Memphis, USA, before returning to the English game with Millwall in January 1983. He also played for Leyton Orient.

STUART, GRAHAM. Exquisite midfielder, whose touch and balance were those of a player destined for greater things. Graham Stuart signed through the youth team and made appearances for England Youth and the England U21 side. He was sold to Everton in August 1993 as the Merseyside club needed a midfield player with grit and determination as well as finesse. He has played nearly every game since his move, and his silky skills have gone down a treat at Goodison Park.

STUBBS, LESLIE. Inside-forward who first signed for Southend United from local league side, Great Wakering, in May 1948. He made 84 league appearances and scored 40 goals which alerted just about every major club in the land to his presence and ability. Chelsea signed him in November 1952 and had found themselves a hard-grafting and amenable striker who could hit a ball equally as accurately with either foot, hence his high goal tally at Southend. In a six-season spell at Stamford Bridge he made 112 league appearances and scored 34 goals. Stubbs later moved back to Southend in November 1958.

SUART, RONALD. Team manager October 1974 – April 1975. Cumbrian-born centre-half, Suart made his footballing debut with Netherfield, moving to Blackpool in January 1939. He later played for Blackburn Rovers, before a role as player/manager at Wigan Athletic in September 1955, which lasted just one year when he left to take over at Scunthorpe United, then Blackpool. He arrived at Stamford Bridge in April 1967 as assistant manager to Tommy

Graham Stuart

Docherty, and, for a brief spell in October of that year, found himself temporarily in charge of the team, until Dave Sexton was brought in to take over.

In October 1974, he was given the opportunity he had been waiting for, a crack at the Chelsea job, but he had a tough task ahead of him as Sexton's side were strong candidates for relegation. When they were relegated in April 1975, Suart stood down as manager and took over the role of general manager, a position he held until 1978. This pleasant Cumbrian remained at Chelsea until 1983 as chief coach. A fair manager, he never quite instilled the confidence and motivation required after the departure of Sexton.

SWAIN, KENNETH. Tough right-back Kenny Swain was picked up from Wycombe Wanderers in August 1973 and proved to be a player of outstanding quality. Although capable of playing a physical game, he much preferred to use his ball control and neat passing movements to challenge the opposition.

Swain quickly established himself in the team and made 127 appearances between 1973 and 1978 when he was sold to Aston Villa. He later played for Nottingham Forest, Portsmouth, West Bromwich Albion, and Crewe Alexandria, notching up well over 600 appearances in total. A totally dedicated professional and dependable defender for every one of his clubs, he has Chelsea to thank for setting him off on the road to a fine career.

T

TAMBLING, ROBERT. Words cannot sufficiently describe
how good this footballer was as a striker and goal scorer.
Few players of any era earn the ultimate respect of a club's
support, who can at times be remarkably fickle. The mere
mention of Bobby Tambling's name has all Chelsea fans
going into raptures about his goals and his all-round ability.
He is a true Chelsea hero.

Born in Storrington, Sussex, in 1941, Robert Victor
Tambling represented his school side, appropriately named,
Storrington School. Whilst still a schoolboy he was called
up into the England Schoolboy International squad, making
his debut against Ireland in 1956. He gained further
honours at schoolboy level against Eire, Wales (twice),
Ireland, Scotland and Germany in 1957. He joined Chelsea
as part of the apprentice scheme which involved him
sweeping the terracing and cleaning the first-team players'
boots. He signed professional for the Blues in September
1958 and made his first-team debut on 7 February 1959 in
a home fixture against West Ham United which Chelsea
won 3–2. Bobby netted once, displaying his desire for goals
to over 53,000 spectators who had packed the ground.
Anyone present on that day will recall the buzz that went
through the crowd each time Tambling received the ball in

the Hammers' half, it was clear from the outset that he was as dangerous a marksman as Chelsea had ever had.

He made 366 appearances and scored 202 goals, many of them solo efforts. Tambling's ethos was quite simple, take the most direct route to goal and score, it was the keeper's job to stop him, but as he had the ball the keeper had to do all the work. Time and again some of the country's greatest shot-stoppers found themselves picking the ball out of their net after Tambling had struck. He was probably the most complete forward the club have ever had, including Jimmy Greaves, which is acclaim of the highest order, well-deserved by a player who brought so much joy and contentment to the Stamford Bridge faithful. In January 1970, after a brief loan spell, he signed for Crystal Palace, Dave Sexton believing that as he had matured he had lost some of that awesome pace which used to leave defenders in his wake. The loss of pace coincided with a drop in the goal tally. He remained at Palace until 1973 when he appeared for a number of Irish clubs. He was capped 3 times at England full International level, these came in 1963 against France and Wales, and in 1966 against Yugoslavia. It remains one of the greatest mysteries in football why Sir Alf Ramsey never selected him as a regular England player.

TELEVISION. Chelsea appeared in two of the first five *Match of the Day* programmes, then shown on BBC2. The show was initially confined to the London area only. The games featured were against Sunderland on 29 August 1964 (the second ever programme) and against Leeds United on 19 September 1964 (the fifth ever programme). As a matter of interest the Blues won both games, 3–1 v Sunderland and 2–0 v Leeds.

TELEVISION AUDIENCE. The 1970 FA Cup Final between Chelsea and Leeds United attracted the biggest television viewing audience of the whole of the 1970s when some 32 million people watched the thrilling 2–2 draw at Wembley on 11 April 1970.

TENNANT, ALBERT. Wing-half signed from Stanton Iron Works in November 1934 at the age of 17. Tennant was a typical wing-half, stocky and tough in the tackle. His career was badly disrupted by the war years. He made just 2 league appearances thereafter. Later he took over as coach at the club.

TERNENT, STANLEY. Tough-tackling and resilient right-half whose football career was learnt the hard way because Stan played much of his game with the less fashionable clubs. He signed for Burnley from the ranks of the apprentices in June 1963 before joining Carlisle United in May 1968. At Brunton Park he was a regular first-team player making the number 4 shirt his own. After 186 league appearances for the Cumbrians, he moved to Sunderland. In 1979 he took a coaching role at Blackpool taking over as team manager when the club was struggling to find form and dropping down the table like a lead weight. He enjoyed further spells as assistant manager with Bradford City and Crystal Palace before taking over as manager of Hull City in November 1989, a position he held until January 1991. A short time later he joined Chelsea as assistant to Ian Porterfield. Ternent possesses a marvellous knowledge of the game and has been unfortunate in his full-time managerial roles.

THAIN, ALBERT. Locally-born centre-forward who signed for the club at the beginning of the 1922/23 season. Thain had made excellent progress in the local league sides and reserves and was drafted in as a direct replacement for the great Jack Cock. Thain proved his worth and was a proficient goalscorer for the Blues over the next few seasons.

THOMAS, MICHAEL. Welsh International utility player, who generally plays midfield or as a striker. Micky has, during his often turbulent career, been a real character in the game. His football career began with Wrexham in 1972 where he made a real name for himself as a dynamo in the side's midfield. November 1978 saw a dream move to Manchester United where he made 90 appearances for the Old Trafford side scoring 11 goals before moving to Everton in August 1981. Three months later he found himself at Brighton and Hove Albion, then at Stoke City in August 1982.

His Chelsea career followed, in January 1984 to be precise, when he was reunited with an old manager, in the shape of John Neal who had guided his career at Wrexham. Neal placed a great deal of faith in Thomas and, it has to be said, this was not misplaced. The Welshman produced the kind of form which had seen him move to Manchester United earlier in his career. He was a revelation, with neat passing and control and bags of experience. Unfortunately he was rather injury-prone and was often out of the side for lengthy periods. His return was always welcomed by the Chelsea faithful when his name was read out over the public address system. When John Neal parted from the club, new manager, John Hollins, could see no place for Thomas in his side so released him. Micky made 53 outings for the club and scored 11 goals. He later played for West Bromwich Albion, Derby County, Wichita (USA), Shrewsbury Town, Leeds United, Stoke City and finally, a return to Wrexham. His fine career has been slightly blemished by his activities away from the game, but he will always be remembered with great affection by not only the support of Chelsea, but by football fans in general.

THOMPSON, CHARLES. 'Chick' Thompson, goalkeeper, was signed from Scottish club side, Clyde in October 1952 and was drafted straight into the first eleven. A rather ordinary goalkeeper he was, I suppose, best described as safe and steady, rather than spectacular. To be fair he was playing in a side which was undergoing a great deal of rebuilding and so many players were tried out. He was a slimline keeper who was unusually strong for a man of his build. He made a total of 46 league appearances but struggled to oust Robertson in the Chelsea goal. Thompson was eventually released in August 1957 to Nottingham Forest where he demonstrated some reliability and made 121 league appearances for the East Midlands side.

THOMPSON, JAMES. A Glaswegian who joined the club in January 1965 from Provanside Hibernian. Thompson was a hardy defender who would chase after wingers and run them into the ground. His style was less than spectacular, but he was effective when intercepting passes and breaking down flowing attacks. He made a total of 40 appearances for the Blues and scored one goal. He transferred to Burnley in September 1968 where he became a long-serving and reliable defender with more than 290 league appearances for the Turf Moor side.

TINDALL, RONALD. Big Ron was once the striking partner of Jimmy Greaves, his deft touch in the air provided many of Greaves' goal opportunities. This gifted targetman was something of an all-round sportsman as he played first-class cricket for Surrey during the summer. Tindall arrived at Stamford Bridge as an apprentice and signed for the club in April 1953. He scored on his first-team debut against West Bromwich Albion at Stamford Bridge in November 1955 and looked set for a regular first-team place. His aerial power was his great strength, as he outjumped just about everyone who challenged him. The flick-on was his speciality, although he was equally capable of bringing the ball down to his feet and holding it up for a colleague to run onto. The majority of his 70 goals for Chelsea, however, did come from his head. When he had the ball at his feet he looked cumbersome and about to fall over.

A character in the Chelsea side, he took over the mantle as emergency goalkeeper and defender, being forced to appear in these positions in competitive matches. He made 174 appearances for the club, moving to West Ham United in November 1961. He later played for Reading, and Portsmouth, and represented the English Football League.

TOWNROW, JACK. Dominant centre-half who signed from Clapton Orient in the 1928/29 season and who was to prove a fine signing for the club. Townrow was outstanding in the air, not only did his headers possess power, but there was long-distance accuracy too; equally as good as a pass made with the foot.

TREBLE TRANSFER. Alan Birchenall became the first ever professional footballer in the United Kingdom to be transferred three times for a fee of £100,000, from Sheffield United to Chelsea, in November 1967, from Chelsea to Crystal Palace, in June 1970 and finally, from Crystal Palace to Leicester City in September 1971!

TOWNSEND, ANDREW. Born in Maidstone, Kent, Andy's career began with non-league Weymouth where, as a master 'Terras' midfield he dictated the style of games and was a most influential player. Signed by Southampton in January 1985 he worked hard to build a reputation for himself at the Dell. In 77 league performances, he scored 5 goals but proved, as time progressed, to be improving with virtually every game. Norwich City were the next club to seek out his services and he moved to East Anglia in August 1988. It was here that his educated left foot matured and the rest of the football world sat up and took notice of his exploits on the field of play. Some 66 league appearances and 8 goals were notched up at Carrow Road, before he agreed to join Chelsea in July 1990.

At Stamford Bridge he became one of the finest midfield players of recent times, with a hardened spirit which rubbed off onto his colleagues. Andy was a player whom a team could be built around.

With his never-say-die ethos, he reaped the rewards of never giving up, when in a 1st Division fixture against Leeds United in November 1992, he scored the vital winning goal in the very last minute of play, having created the move from the half-way line. Andy was a well-loved genius at the Bridge and was a player who was always going to attract big money as the transfer speculation grew and grew. After 138 appearances and 19 goals, he left Chelsea for Aston Villa in 1993, and has continued to improve, scoring some sensational goals, such as the strike at Ipswich in the early stages of the 1994/95 season when he bent the ball from 30 yards into the top corner of the net. A Republic of Ireland International he has made well over 40 full International caps; a figure that is still rising and will continue to do so for many seasons to come.

Andy Townsend

TRANSFER RECORD. The English football league transfer record was smashed in November 1947 when Notts County paid £20,000 for the Blues centre-forward Tommy Lawton. Today, a conservative estimate of what Lawton would be worth in the transfer market would be somewhere in the region of £7 million–£10 million!

TUCK, PETER. Inside-forward who made a name for himself in the junior side. Signing for the club in June 1951 he was very much a one-season wonder, as all of his 3 league

177

appearances took place in the 1951/52 season, complete with one league goal. At the age of 19 he had a lot to learn, a difficult task for any youngster in a side undergoing major rebuilding work, and too much for Tuck, I am afraid, as he never played another league game for the club.

U

UPTON, FRANK. Frank 'The Tank' as he was affectionately known, was a midfielder-cum-striker, as well as an accomplished wing-half. His first club was Nuneaton Borough followed by a transfer to Northampton Town in March 1953. At the Cobblers he was possibly the star man, turning in outstanding performances each week. He was a fan's favourite for his aggressive style of tackling and ingenious passing movements, of a type and style never before witnessed with such class at the County Ground. Sadly the price of such fame proved too much for Northampton to keep hold of him and in June 1954, Upton moved to Derby County. In August 1961, The Tank moved to Stamford Bridge in a transfer believed to be around the £15,000 mark. Some 86 appearances were made with 3 goals being scored, between his move and a transfer back to Derby County in September 1965. The Tank played a solid defensive role in the Blues promotion to the 1st division in the 1962/63 season, indeed it was during this same season that he proved his versatility, playing as a striker when called upon to do so. Later he played for Notts County and Worcester City before taking over as player/manager of Workington from January to July 1978 when the Reds finished second from bottom of the 4th division. He has been acting as coach at several clubs since then, and enjoyed a spell as assistant manager with Coventry City between 1985 and 1987. He is a well-versed man in the tactics and styles of football on a national and International level.

V

VENABLES, TERENCE. Born in London's East End this lively inside-forward started his playing days with Dagenham schools before becoming a Chelsea apprentice in July 1958, eventually turning professional in August 1960. As a schoolboy he appeared for his country (England), against Eire, Ireland, Wales, West Germany and Scotland. A distinguished young star he looked set, at a very early age, for a bright future in the game. In those early days his attacking play as enhanced by his skill at crafting opportunities for his colleagues. However, he was a tireless workhorse who was always keen to get back into a defensive role to break down attacks and build them for his own side. He was re-positioned to half-back/wing-half, a move which proved a huge success. By October 1964, Venables had entered the football record books as the first footballer to represent England at five different levels; Schoolboy, Amateur, Youth, U23, and full International. He only represented England at full International level twice in 1964 against Belgium and Holland.

He made a total of 237 appearances for the Blues and scored 31 goals before an £80,000 move to neighbours and London rivals, Tottenham Hotspur in May 1966. He won a League Cup final winners medal in 1965 when Chelsea beat

Leicester City over two legs. The move to Tottenham was not, as has always been believed, a huge success, many of the Spurs fans disliked his style of play and refused to accept him as a player of any real quality. To be fair, he was playing alongside the likes of Greaves, Gilzean, Mackay, Mullery, Jennings and Co.; it would have taken some footballer to match such stars, Terry was not that type of player. Consequently he never seemed to progress in his career at White Hart Lane, although he did win an FA Cup final winners medal when Spurs met Chelsea in the 1967 final and beat them 2–1. In June 1969 he moved to Queen's Park Rangers for £70,000, then on to Crystal Palace in September 1974, taking over as coach, then manager in June 1976 where his young side were tipped as being 'the team of the Eighties'. They ultimately failed to live up to expectations, and Venables left, taking over at Queen's Park Rangers in October 1980, until May 1984 when he moved to Barcelona. His return to England in November 1987, and back to White Hart Lane was hailed as a fantastic achievement by Spurs. In essence it was. Venables had amassed a small fortune from business ventures and was in a good position to financially assist the club. He took over as Chief Executive in July 1991 until an internal feud with club Chairman Alan Sugar dragged the club through the courts and produced nothing but adverse publicity and embarrassment for the club and its supporters.

A tremendous coach and analyst, Venables enjoyed nothing more than the attention of the media circus. A television football pundit, he won over many with his cautious comments and respectful criticism upon the state of the English game, especially the national team. The media circus which worked against so many England managers was used by an astute Venables to his benefit as his reputation as a coach and potential successor to Graham Taylor as England manager began to gain momentum. Eventually, he was given the job. As to whether he is, in fact, the right man for the job, only time will tell. To date, against inferior opposition his sides have failed to inspire although they are notching him up some creditable victories. The 1996 European Championship will be his first real test and already the nation is becoming restless as to who will feature in his team selection.

VICTORY. Chelsea's largest ever victory in first-class competition was against Jeunesse Hautcharage at Stamford Bridge on 29 September 1971, 13–0, in the European Cup Winners Cup competition.

VICTORY. The club's record league victory stands at 9–2, on 1 September 1906, when they overpowered Glossop North End in a football league 2nd Division fixture.

VICTORY. The club's record victory in the FA Cup competition stands at 9–1, achieved on 11 January 1908 in the first round of the competition at Stamford Bridge, against Worksop Town.

VICTORY CUP. A competition held after the end of the First World War, purely for London-based clubs. The final was held at Highbury Stadium and featured Chelsea and Fulham. Chelsea ran out easy winners 3–0. Two came from the cultured feet of Jock Rutherford, officially an Arsenal player, but guesting for the club during the wartime period. Another outstanding talent on the day was Bolton Wanderers magician, Ted Vizard, also guesting for the club and who ran the Fulham defence ragged. The victory ensured that Chelsea had won their first ever cup, but it was not about the winning, more the fact that football could continue with an air of normality now the hostilities had ceased.

VILJOEN, COLIN. A quality midfielder whose playing career began in his home country, South Africa. Signed by Ipswich Town in March 1967 Viljoen soon proved himself to be a player of some distinction, with a passing ability that could split defences open or create space and movements for his wide men. The passing game was not his only attribute, as he was a capable dribbler and a creative artist with the ball at his feet, with a speciality of bending shots towards goal. He made some 305 appearances for Ipswich Town, scoring

45 goals, before a transfer to Manchester City in August 1978. The move to Maine Road was not initially a huge success, so in March 1980, after playing just 27 games for the Maine Road side he moved to Stamford Bridge where Geoff Hurst placed great faith in his undoubted talent. Although 32 years old, Viljoen was still capable of running at defences, his passing game had, if anything, improved. Now playing 2nd Division football, he seemed to adapt to the space but not to the physical challenge of the game. Colin, after a great start, failed to mark his influence on the side and was eventually released in the summer of 1982, when manager John Neal felt that there was no future for him at the Bridge.

An England International, he gained 2 full caps against Nigeria and Wales in 1975. He made 22 first-team appearances for Chelsea, with one further as substitute, without scoring a goal.

W

WALDRON, COLIN. Larger-than-life central-defender, Colin Waldron was first noticed by Lancashire side, Bury who picked him from the obscurity of the non-league game and introduced him to their league eleven in 1966. Just 20 league appearances later and this talented defender was on the move, this time to Stamford Bridge, signing in July 1967. Waldron was a defender who would take no nonsense, his ability to tackle and clear the ball from danger was at times frustrating. Yes, his defensive skills were good, but all too often the ball was hoofed clear and straight back to the opposition allowing them to rebuild their attack. He made just 10 appearances in three months for Chelsea before being sold to Burnley in October 1967.

At Turf Moor he matured and became a defender of real quality. Outstanding performances earned him the team captain's role. In 1976 he moved to Manchester United, then on to Sunderland, before a spell abroad with Atlanta in the USA. He eventually returned to England to play with Rochdale. Colin Waldron was, effectively, the one that got away, had he remained at Stamford Bridge he would no doubt have been challenging for regular first-team football and would have probably become the mainstay of the side.

WALKER, CLIVE. For a left-winger, Clive Walker was rather stout and hardly the usual shape or size. Yet, give him the ball at his feet and he was off, flying down the left wing like a leopard after its prey. Cutting inside and out he would often run straight through to the goal and fire a shot home with consummate ease. An England schoolboy International he signed for Chelsea as an apprentice, signing full-time in May 1975. He made 191 appearances and scored 61 goals, with some spectacular volleys in his repertoire. Clive could be brilliant on his day, then again he could be mundane and seem to lack motivation. His crossing was not his best quality nor was his distribution, but few could forget the sight of him attacking defenders, weaving in and out, jinking and swaying before delivering the ball into the penalty area. He was sold to Sunderland in July 1984, then played for Queen's Park Rangers, Fulham and Brighton and Hove Albion. He now plays his football with Woking in the GM Vauxhall Conference, and still possesses that little bit of extra ball control and skill which puts him above the average non-league player.

WALKER, THOMAS. Tommy first played for Chelsea as a guest player in the 1944/45 season, he then served overseas with the Royal Corps of Signals and it seemed that Chelsea had seen the last of the man whose career began in Scotland with Heart of Midlothian in 1932. As a youngster he quickly established himself in the Tynecastle side's first eleven and gained full International recognition in 1935; this was to be the first of 21 full caps he won. Clearly, active service in the Second World War spoiled his outstanding football career, but the guest appearances for Chelsea were of great satisfaction to both him and those fans who witnessed his educated feet defying all logic as he wiggled, flicked and tapped the ball past, through, and around anyone who thought they could dispossess him.

Walker was brought back to Chelsea in September 1946 when manager Billy Birrell decided that he was the one man in the game he wanted to play for his side. The Chelsea support rejoiced when he returned to Stamford Bridge as a regular Chelsea player. Tommy was a revelation, his play on the field earned him great praise from pundits and critics alike and his attitude off the field was genuine and honest. He would do anything for anyone, realising that he was no different to anyone else, he acknowledged supporters wherever he was and would gladly converse with them. A true ambassador for the game and his club, it was almost too good to be true. He made over 100 appearances for the Blues and scored 24 goals before returning to Heart of Midlothian as player/manager in January 1949. He left many broken hearts behind as Chelsea was sad to see him leave. Few footballers of his kind are still remembered in the modern era, yet Tommy Walker OBE is one whose skill and judgment remain unquestionable, a man of impeccable character and a real hero into the bargain. He sadly passed away in Edinburgh in 1993.

WARREN, BENJAMIN. Right-half signed from Derby County in 1908 and who was forced to retire from the game through illness just three years later. Warren was born in Derbyshire and first played for Newhall Town before promotion to the town's senior side, Newhall Swifts. It was with Swifts that Derby first noticed his talents in the tackle and distribution. Having signed for the Rams he matured to become one of the best right-halfs of his time, making 11 appearances for the England full International side between 1906 and 1911. There was also the honour of appearing in an FA Cup Final for Derby in 1903 which they lost 6–0 to Bury.

WARREN, ROBERT. Born in Devonport, Plymouth, in 1927, Warren joined his local league club, Plymouth Argyle from Plymouth United in February 1946. A centre-half, he made just 3 league appearances for the Home Park side before signing for Chelsea in July 1948. Unfortunately he never quite made the grade at Stamford Bridge, the central defender's role was not to be his as he struggled to match the pace of the game and was something of a lumbering giant. In August 1951 he returned to the South West with Torquay United.

WATSON, IAN. Ian Watson was, after he left Stamford Bridge, one of the most established full-backs in the English game. He initially signed through the Chelsea junior set up in February 1962, but, like all youngsters attempting to break into the first team, he found it difficult to sufficiently impress whilst playing at a lower standard. He did manage 9 appearances and actually scored a goal but this was insufficient to keep him at the club. Queen's Park Rangers signed him in July 1965 and he remained at Loftus Road for the rest of his professional playing career in England, injury robbing him of an extended run. He retired from Rangers in 1973. A solid and reliable defender, he was compatible in a sound Rangers side and was often used as a utility player. At Chelsea he was confined to the defender's role and to be fair, although he lacked lengthy pace, he rarely put a foot wrong at the Bridge, the same is true of his career at QPR.

WEAVER, SAMUEL. England International wing-half who first played for Sutton Town in 1926 before joining Hull City in March 1928. He then joined Newcastle United in November 1929 making 204 league appearances for the Geordies before moving to Stamford Bridge in August 1936.

A ferocious tackler and vindictive attacker Sammy Weaver was a driving force behind the Chelsea side, as he constantly hassled his own colleagues to work hard and show more commitment. He was synonymous with the long throw, as he would launch the ball into the air where it would remain for what seemed an eternity before dropping a good distance from where he stood. His Chelsea career was badly disrupted with the intervention of the Second World War and when this was over, he remained for just a short time, before signing for Stockport County in December 1947 where he ended his playing days. He later acted as coach/trainer at Leeds United, then Millwall, before moving back to the Midlands with Mansfield Town in 1955 where he remained in several posts until 1971, including, manager, coach, caretaker manager, trainer and scout. His England career saw him gain 3 full International caps between 1932/33.

WEBB, DAVID. Mr Chelsea, David Webb was an infectious character yet gave the impression of being rather dour and apathetic. A tall, thick-set player his appearance alone commands respect, his football style was slightly less oppressive. Webb began with West Ham United as an amateur before joining Leyton Orient in May 1963. After three seasons at Brisbane Road he moved to Southampton where he developed very nicely and produced many solid and determined performances as a central defender.

In February 1968 he arrived at Stamford Bridge, keen to make an impression and he did just that. Powerful and stiff, he dominated the Chelsea defence with his aerial combat and strength on the ground. He was a master of his trade. He made some 298 appearances and scored 44 goals, none more important than the winner against Leeds United in the 1970 FA Cup final replay at Old Trafford, when the ball was forced home by his right shoulder, neck and ear. Not pretty but typical of his game; strong and hard. Webby was sold to Queen's Park Rangers in July 1974, and later played for Leicester City, Derby County and Bournemouth, there was even a spell as a non-contract player/manager. He returned to Chelsea in February 1993 as manager, in an attempt to halt a slide which had seen the club slip perilously close to the relegation zone in the 1st Division. Webby was given a three-month contract to prove himself, and where previously he had worked wonders at Torquay United, Bournemouth and Southend, here was a chance to haul a big club back into the big time. His football tactics were not pleasing, indeed they were rough and often reckless, but Webby certainly got the team working as a unit and, more importantly, put some passion and desire into their commitment to play for Chelsea. At the end of the season, Chelsea finished mid-table and everyone expected David Webb to be announced as the permanent manager. Instead he left, and Glenn Hoddle took over. Webby will be long remembered and respected as a star of the Chelsea team, as a manager he undoubtedly helped the club's cause and deserves a great deal of credit for what he achieved.

WEGERLE, ROY. When Roy Wegerle joined Chelsea from Tampa Bay Rowdies in June 1986 many a club manager and supporter turned up their noses and laughed at Chelsea for signing an American import. Wegerle has since made them eat their words as he has proved himself to be a consistent goalscorer at the highest level. At Chelsea he was very much a raw youngster eager to impress and keen to please everyone, yet he had that vicious instinct in front of goal which saw him net 4 goals in 18 first-team appearances for Chelsea. A loan spell with Swindon Town in 1988 expanded

Roy Wegerle

his experience but not sufficiently for Chelsea to realise his full potential. Roy had to go; quite simply, he was a luxury they could ill afford to keep in their reserves so he was sold to Luton Town in July 1988. He later played for Queen's Park Rangers, where he won goal of the season for a wonderful effort at Leeds when he beat five men before slotting the ball neatly into the bottom corner of the net. He then moved to Blackburn Rovers before Coventry City signed him in 1992.

WELLER, KEITH. When asked a few years ago which professional footballer used to wear tights to keep warm when playing, I instinctively responded with 'Keith Weller'. I can still see him wearing the black hosiery and seemingly revelling in the attention his crazy appearance was attracting. This aside, Keith Weller was a very experienced and extremely talented professional footballer. Signed by Tottenham Hotspur as a youngster, he progressed to make 19 league appearances for Spurs and score one goal before moving to South London with Millwall in June 1967. It was at the Den that he earned his reputation for possessing a piledriver of a shot, and being a marvellous distributor of the ball from deep in the Lions' midfield.

He arrived at Chelsea in May 1970 eager to prove his ability at the highest level, sadly his dream was never realised. Despite making 48 appearances and bagging 15 goals, Keith never truly settled in at the Bridge. He possessed a beautiful pass, and was creative enough, but somehow he lacked that little extra magic which had served Millwall so rewardingly. Thus, when Leicester City came in for him in September 1971, Keith was allowed to leave. He remained at Filbert Street for 7 years as a player, scoring 37 league goals in 260 games. He received International recognition with England, winning 4 full caps against Wales, Nigeria, Scotland and Argentina in 1974.

WEMBLEY. Chelsea have appeared in first class competitive finals on four occasions, winning just once and that was after a replay at Old Trafford, Manchester. For the record, the finals consist of three FA Cup and one League Cup. Full

Colin West

Members and Zenith Data Cup competitions are not included, although the club won these at Wembley in 1986 and 1990 respectively.

WEST, COLIN. Striker signed as an apprentice and who turned professional in September 1985. Colin West's was not an illustrious career at Chelsea; just 8 games and 4 goals for a forward who stood at just 5′ 8″. He possessed, at times, some exhilarating pace but was a little too easily knocked from the ball. He had spells with Partick Thistle and Swansea City before leaving the Blues for Dundee in 1990, he is currently playing with Hartlepool United.

WHIFFEN, KINGSLEY. Goalkeeper signed as an apprentice who never quite made the grade for the club. He made one first-team appearance in 1966, aged just 16, but was never again called upon to represent the first eleven.

WHITE, ALEXANDER. When Alexander White signed from Bonnyrigg Rose in February 1937 much was expected of his stylish counter-attacking play down the right wing. An unusually quick-thinking full-back he could have equally been at home in the midfield role. Then, with the advent of wartime, football was badly disrupted, as was Alex's Chelsea career. He made just 17 appearances for the club, all after the war but by this stage had lost a little of his old sparkle. He was transferred to Swindon Town in July 1948 and later played for Southport.

WHITTAKER, RICHARD. Republic of Ireland International defender and 'B' International player. Signed from St Mary's Boys Club, Dublin in May 1952. He was more of a squad player than a first-team regular but made 51 appearances without a goal between 1952 and October 1960 when he moved to Peterborough United. He also played for Queen's Park Rangers.

WICKS, STANLEY. A fine centre-half who hailed from Reading in Berkshire. Wicks was strong and hefty in the challenge, his greatest season at the Bridge being the 1954/55 Championship year. In a career that began with Reading in August 1948 before the dream move to Chelsea in January 1954, Stan forced his way to recognition with some determined displays in the reserves and second string. Once he had managed to appear for the first eleven he was difficult to oust, as his ferocity and enthusiastic aggression were serious contributors to Chelsea's success that season. He made a total of 80 appearances for the club and scored one goal. He received recognition for England at 'B' level, with one cap, he also represented the Football League.

WICKS, STEPHEN. Signed as an apprentice at Stamford Bridge and graduated to make England Youth and U21 International appearances. 'Wicksy' was a giant of a centre-half, robust, uncompromising, yet articulate with the ball. He let his feet and head do the talking, with some intelligent forward-passing play. First signed for the club in June 1974 and made his full first-team debut at Stamford Bridge on 10 January 1975 in a 3–0 defeat at the hands of Oldham Athletic. Steve Wicks grew in stature but was, unfortunately, author of his own downfall at Chelsea. He was one of the most consistent players in the first team so when money was required to rebuild the side, it was Wicksy who went, to Derby County in January 1979. After a spell with Derby he transferred to Queen's Park Rangers, then to Crystal Palace before returning to Loftus Road in March 1982. He returned to Chelsea in July 1986, but was hardly the player everyone recalled so affectionately. Eventually, having suffered the despair of being dropped from the first team, Steve was forced to retire from the game through a back problem, making a career total of 163 games for the Blues, with 8 goals.

WILKINS, GRAHAM. Brother of the current Queen's Park Rangers manager, Ray Wilkins. Graham signed for Chelsea through the apprentice scheme signing professional forms in July 1972 some 15 months before his brother was to do the same thing. A full-back, he was determined and possessed a neat first touch, yet there was a certain lack of composure when the going got tough. His efforts in creating attacks from a defensive role were noteworthy, especially when given the freedom to roam down the wing.

He made just 148 appearances and scored one goal in ten seasons at the Bridge. Struggling to meet with any sort of consistent form, he was in and out of the team on a regular basis. Despite this he gave everything he had for Chelsea. He moved to Brentford in July 1982.

WILKINS, RAYMOND. What can one say about this player which has not been said before. 'Butch' has had an incredible football career, which will come as no surprise to those who witnessed him as a boy at Stamford Bridge. Signed in October 1973, he went on to make 193 appearances for the Blues and scored 34 goals. His career has also seen him appear at Schoolboy, Youth, Under 21, Under 23, and full International levels for England where he has attained 84 caps. A midfield player, his awareness, control and vision have seldom been bettered in the modern game. Add to this an exemplary attitude and total commitment and you have one of the most complete footballers of all time. His one failing is in his height; one of the few ways of getting past him was by punting the ball high over his head and running past him. Not as easy as it sounds, as Ray could turn and pounce as quick as any predator observing its quarry.

It was clear from the outset that he was content at Stamford Bridge and it would take something special to draw him away. That something special was the need for extra finances at the club which were readily supplied by Manchester United in part exchange for the services of this Blues favourite. The move took place in August 1979 for a fee of £375,000, creating uproar on the terraces as fans fumed over his departure. To this day he is still recalled with great affection, his skill on the ball will long remain in the memory of most football fans. Long-range shots, curled passes, or just plain old determined tackling, Butch had the lot.

He joined Glasgow Rangers after his spell at Old Trafford, before returning to London with Queen's Park Rangers and then a brief move to Crystal Palace. He returned to Loftus Road in the early stages of the 1994/95 season as manager, clearly a contender for greater things in this role. Fans now taunt Butch with cries of 'slaphead', a measure of his maturity and how the fans, two decades after he turned professional, still feel it necessary to identify him as a character. His attitude and philosophy today have hardly changed from when he was a boy at Chelsea all those years ago, keep it simple, and do the easy things. I doubt if Ray will find another like himself for a long, long time.

WILLEMSE, STANLEY. Born in Brighton, Stan joined his local league side in June 1946 and progressed to make 91 league appearances for the Seagulls. A solid and dependable left-back he possessed a cultured left foot, which was all too effective at knocking a ball past a challenger as Stan tucked in his shoulders and darted through the tackle. He signed for Chelsea in July 1949 and was a dependable and rugged character who never let the side down especially during the Championship season of 1954/55. June 1956 saw his departure to Leyton Orient as the glorious Champions were ripped apart in poor defence of their title the following season. Stan made appearances for England at Schoolboy, and 'B' International level, he also represented the Football League. He appeared in 220 competitive fixtures for Chelsea, and scored 2 goals.

WILLIAMS, PAUL. Apprentice who was signed through the apprentice scheme and who made just one appearance for the first team. That was at Boundary Park, Oldham, on April 1983 when he appeared as centre-half.

WILLIAMS, REGINALD. Inside-forward signed from Watford as an amateur in October 1945. Reg was a wily campaigner blessed with some neat footwork and close-control ball skills. The dropping of a shoulder to get past your man was displayed by him with extreme confidence and purpose. He was at his best in tight situations, with defenders snapping at his heels. Here, Reg seemed in his element, holding off the challenge and twisting and turning this way and that. He made some 38 league appearances with 13 goals between 1945 and 1951.

WILSON, ANDREW. Signed from Middlesbrough in November 1923, Andy Wilson cost the club a then record fee of £6,500 and was a Scotland International, as well as captain of the side. His favoured role was that of attacking midfielder; following in behind the centre-forward and behind the two wingers he liked nothing more than to collect the ball being cleared in front of him, looking to his wide men, and playing a perfectly-weighted through ball for a cross or a shot. A footballer whose talents were not hampered by a badly disabled left arm, his finger joints being restricted in their movement as a result of an old war wound. Andy showed how disabilities can be overcome, as he regularly maintained a single-figure handicap at golf and was a fine player of bowls. Standing at just over 5′ 6″ his diminutive figure was enhanced by a strong, muscular build which allowed him to challenge with the biggest of players, his skill often proving too much for his opponent. Andy moved to Queen's Park Rangers after eight seasons with Chelsea, he then played for a brief time in France, with Nimes. He was later manager of Walsall but disliked the managerial role at Fellows Park.

WILSON, CLIVE. Defender who could also act as cover in left-wing positions. Clive was quick, very quick. In fact, he was that quick that he would often lose himself! All too often, with the ball at his feet, he would set off on a forward run, zipping past the opposition until an opening appeared, it was then that his play often became calamitous; the ball which he had majestically stroked before him, suddenly became entangled between his feet like a lead weight, and Clive, in an effort to regain composure would slow down, lose concentration and either leave the ball behind or trip over it. Having said that, he is now one of the most composed players in the Premier League, so the experience of 16 years in the top flight has served him well.

His career began with Manchester City in 1979 before a move to Chelsea in May 1987 after a brief loan spell with Chester City in 1982. At the Bridge he made 85 appearances and scored 5 goals before being sold to Queen's Park Rangers in July 1990.

WILSON, KEVIN. If determination and endeavour were part and parcel of every footballers' make-up then Kevin Wilson would be the prince of them all. Although slight in build he possessed nerves of steel and 'got stuck in' whenever the need arose. A confident player, he could strike the ball with some accuracy from long distances, his shooting prowess was equally as impressive so it comes as no surprise that he gained some 27 full International caps for Northern Ireland.

Kevin first played for Banbury United before signing for Derby County in December 1979. A move to Ipswich followed before Chelsea took him into their fold in June 1987. One-hundred-and-fifty-five appearances with 55 goals speaks volumes for the player's ability to meet with the high demands placed upon him. In March 1992 he was sold to Notts County, before moving again, this time to Walsall, where he is part of the management but still plays in the first team.

WINDRIDGE, JAMES. An England International inside-forward signed from Small Heath in April 1905. Jimmy Windridge was one of the top forwards of his time, his skill was not only in taking the opportunities, but creating them for colleagues. He was something of an all-rounder in all sports and played cricket for Warwickshire on 3 occasions between 1909 and 1913. He moved to Middlesbrough in November 1911 having served Chelsea well and later moved to Birmingham City in November 1914 only to retire with the outbreak of the First World War.

WINTER, DANIEL. Full-back signed from Bolton Wanderers in December 1945. Danny had been picked up from local Welsh football appearing for Mais-y-hof. He was one of the stars of the side and had been watched by several league sides. Few players in his position could claim to be consistent performers, indeed, Danny was never an outstanding defender, probably because he was almost inconspicuous in each of his 131 league appearances for the Blues. This clearly suggests that he got on with the job required with little fuss but with a great effectiveness.

WISE, DENNIS. Little Dennis Wise is the current hero of the Chelsea support. Virtually a cult figure, his appetite for the game is infectious and affects everyone who watches him play. Signed as an apprentice at Southampton, he moved to Wimbledon in March 1985 and initially seemed far too small to be effective, yet his energy and desire to win pulled him through those difficult early days. Although a winger,

Dennis Wise

he plays his best football forward of the midfield running on to balls and chasing defenders back towards their own goal. Having made 127 league appearances for the Dons, he signed for Chelsea in July 1990 and was an instant hit with the fans. His precocious talent has been harnessed and is now influenced by the master of midfield, Glen Hoddle. Although the manager still allows Wisey to express himself in his own inimitable style.

An England full International with further honours for his country at U21 and 'B' levels it is easy to see why he is so adored by the Chelsea fans. For a man of his size, he is keen to put himself about, and occasionally oversteps the mark with his enthusiasm getting the better of him. The occasional lapse in self-discipline is his greatest weakness, not that he cannot control it, but it seems every so often that he will make one comment too many to a referee, or clip a players heels just once too often. This antagonises match officials who all too often record his name in their little black books! Despite all of this Dennis is a star, a player who can bring a smile to your face with his antics or flashes of genius on the pitch, which in itself says a great deal about him as a footballer, with very few modern players being able to do so.

WOOD, DARREN. A fine defender and a talented footballer, Darren was first noticed by Middlesbrough who signed him from the non-league game in July 1981. Within three seasons at Ayresome Park he had made 101 league appearances, and was by now attracting the attentions of some of the country's bigger clubs, including Chelsea who signed him in September 1984. At the Bridge he was impressive either in the right-back position or in midfield. Between 1984 and January 1989, when he moved to Sheffield Wednesday, he made 167 appearances for the club, and scored 4 goals.

WOODLEY, VICTOR. When he was described as a goalkeeper who could meet all demands, one realises that Vic Woodley must have been something special and indeed he was. A goalkeeper, who made some 19 full International appearances for England between 1937–1939 and whose appetite for the game was outstanding. He first played for Windsor and Eton before signing for Chelsea in 1931 and replaced the great Sam Millingon between the sticks the following season. Woodley was a real professional who worked and trained hard at improving his game, and although less than spectacular, his performances were acknowledged as being those of the country's best keeper of the 1930s. Curiously, one season after he took over the keeper's mantle at the Bridge, the club signed Scottish

Darren Wood

International goalkeeper, John Jackson, who at once ousted Woodley. Both men trained together and where one might have expected some bitterness, there was none. Woodley eventually regained his place when Jackson fell foul to a nasty injury early in his Chelsea career.

In December 1945, with the war having all but finished his playing days, Vic Woodley was released to Bath City where he kept goal with such panache that Derby County brought him back to league football in March 1946. However, now aged 36, he was past his best in the agility

Victor Woodley

stakes and returned to Bath City as player/manager in 1947, a position he held until December 1947 when he retired from the game and became a pub landlord. Putting it plainly Vic Woodley was undoubtedly one of the best goalkeepers Chelsea has ever had.

WOODWARD, VIVIAN. One of the greatest forwards of the first two decades of the 20th Century. Viv Woodward first played for Tottenham Hotspur in 1901 moving across London to Stamford Bridge in 1909, where his dribbling talents mesmerised fans and opposition alike. An England International he gained 23 caps between 1903 and 1911. He was part of the England amateur squad which toured South Africa in 1910, where he made a further 3 appearances for his country. These statistics were officially disregarded by the Football Association as the tour was classed as 'unofficial'. Politics and football clearly don't mix: who says such problems are those of modern times? Viv retired from playing with the outbreak of the First World War and later became a director of Tottenham Hotspur, then held a similar post at Chelsea from 1922 to 1930.

X

XMAS-DAY FIXTURES. The club's first ever competitive football league fixtures to be held on a Christmas Day took place in the 1906/07 season, with an away 2nd Division fixture at Hull City. The result, a 1–0 win. Well worth the long journey North.

The following season, 1907/08, the first in 1st Division Chelsea again played on Christmas Day and won 4–1 at Liverpool. This was followed the next season by a 2–1 win at Manchester City, before Notts County ended the pleasant run in the 1909/10 season, beating the Blues 2–1. The first ever Christmas Day fixture to be played at Stamford Bridge was in the 1912/13 season when Manchester United were the visitors and ran out 4–1 winners.

Y

YOUNG, ALAN. Centre-half who first played for Arsenal having made his way through the youth set up at Highbury.

He made just 4 first-team appearances for the Gunners before signing for Chelsea in November 1961.

He was something of a reserve/squad player in his time at Stamford Bridge and made just 26 appearances between 1961 and 1966. He later played for Torquay United where he was more of a first-team regular.

YOUNGEST. Jimmy Greaves was just 19 years and 86 days old when he made his England full International debut.

Ron 'Chopper' Harris is the youngest FA Cup Final captain, when in 1967 he was 26 years old.

YOUTH CUP. The 1958 final of the FA Youth Cup is one to be forgotten as far as Chelsea fans are concerned. The finals are two-legged affairs. On this occasion, the Blues faced Wolverhampton Wanderers, the first leg being held at Stamford Bridge. When the final whistle blew after 90 minutes, the competition was virtually over as Chelsea had ended up comfortable 5–1 winners. The second leg at Molineux was disastrous; after 90 minutes the final score was 6–1, to Wolves! So Wanderers won the competition 7–6 on aggregate! It only goes to show that nothing is certain in football.

Z

ZENITH DATA SYSTEMS CUP. Chelsea actually won this competition in the 1989/90 season when they faced Middlesbrough in the Wembley final. In March 1990, some 76,000 fans flocked to the stadium to watch a poor, forgettable match. The only memorable moment was when Tony Dorigo stepped up to strike one of the best goals ever seen in the stadium, when he bent a free-kick from 25 yards around the Boro' wall and into the top corner of the net. Middlesbrough goalkeeper Stephen Pears said afterwards: 'There was no keeper in the world could have got near it, how he done it I will never know.' The final score was, in fact, 1–0 to the Blues. Success in the Nineties, will it end there?

SELECT BIBLIOGRAPHY

A History of Chelsea F.C. Ralph Finn (Pelham Books, 1970)

Rothmans Football Yearbooks 1970–1995 (Queen Anne Press/ Headline)

Daily Mail football guides – numerous seasons

Chelsea, An Illustrated History Scott Cheshire (Breedon Books, 1994)

Soccer Star Magazine

Charles Buchan's *Football Monthly*

Goal

Chelsea FC programmes – too many to mention.

Any one of the above are well worth a read. Although some will be difficult to obtain, may I recommend the Soccer Bookshelf, Cleethorpes, to anyone in need of football books new or old, they are truly top of their league. Thanks, John.